Prayers
THAT BRING
Miracles

Stephen M. Bird

Prayers That Bring Miracles
© 1997 by Stephen M. Bird
All rights reserved

Library of Congress Cataloging-in-Publication Data

Bird, Stephen M., 1949–
Prayers that bring miracles / Stephen M. Bird.
p.   cm.
Includes bibliographical references.
ISBN 1-56236-238-0
1. Church of Jesus Christ of Latter-day Saints—Doctrines.
2. Mormon Church—Doctrines. 3. Prayer—Mormon Church. I. Title.
BX8656.B58   1997
248.3' 2—dc21   97-44694
CIP

5 4 3 2 1

Cover design: Jeanette Andrews
Cover illustration: Keith Larsen

Printed in the United States of America

Prayers

THAT BRING

Miracles

What Readers Are Saying about This Book:

"It was one of the best books that I've ever read.... Prior to reading this book, I had not been praying for quite some time. I just couldn't find the motivation in me.... Reading Brother Bird's book helped to restore my hope, faith, and commitment to daily meaningful prayer. The book is simple, direct, and moving." —Donna Bush, clinical social work

"The reading of this book has reawakened within me the confidence that God does hear and answer our prayers." —Scott Paulson, real estate title examiner

"What a joy it is to read gentle, powerful concepts of truth written so clearly it motivates you to implement and expand them in your life. Seldom one sees scriptures, quotations and thoughts blended so simply and beautifully. Wonderful reading for those tender in the gospel, mature in the gospel, and those who have lost their way. For all who enjoy feeling the gentle touch of the Spirit." —William R. Isham, business owner

Prayers That Bring Miracles is a rare book. . . . [It] brought real hope and comfort to me as I read it. This is *must* reading for anyone wanting to deepen their relationship with Heavenly Father." —Robert Smith, author of *Baptists at Our Barbecue*

"I love this book.... Stephen Bird has created a new format that brings new life to ideas that have been around forever.... I was so full when I finished reading, and I wanted to shared the message of this book." —Darla Hanks Isackson, co-author of *To Parents, with Love*

"Very direct and challenging. The point of view is so immediate and down to earth that prayer is brought away from the mystical and/or 'other guys' experience to being 'right with me.'" —Douglas Eddington, facilities field manager

"Simpy refreshing. A tremendous gift to those who want to learn the simple truths of prayer." —Stacey Bess, author of *Nobody Don't Love Nobody*

"I carry *Prayers That Bring Miracles* right along with my scriptures to read and reread because I find the message rich and rewarding. It is a classic that belongs on everyone's bookshelf regardless of one's denomination or spiritual inclination." —Donna Barnes, counselor

"It changed my life. I've read the book now three times and I've started it again.... [It] brought so many scriptures, stories, and ideas together on a principle that made it 'click' into place. This is the first time I've really felt like I'm talking to someone and that person is listening." —Cheryl McMullin, elementary school teacher

"*Prayers That Bring Miracles* does just what it says. I had never felt the Spirit as strong as when I was reading this book. My whole life has been spent trying to get as close to the Lord as this book has helped me get." —Maury Douglas Wheatley, poet and songwriter

"That book was so powerful to me. I was looking for answers to a medical condition. When I read your book I wept and wept. Your book was an answer to prayer." —Carolyn Hermansen, administrative secretary

"I know now, as I used to when I was active, that God does live and answer prayers.... There are no words to express my thanks. Since reading your book I've received personal revelations, one after another. My husband and I are both active now. Our testimonies are vibrant, and we have been sealed in the temple." —Ann Aitken, homemaker

"What a blast of light! I've read it three times now. This book has changed my prayers! While reading *Prayers That Bring Miracles,* I felt a powerful spirit. I now have the tools and steps I need to know my Heavenly Father." —Pam Wilford, early-morning seminary teacher

"I've read it three times. The Lord has answered so many of my prayers lately. I encourage all people of all denominations to read this book. The Lord will answer your prayers also!" —Cindy Herrera, CNA

Acknowledgments

This book is just one of many miracles our Heavenly Father has made for me. I know the limits of my abilities, and the quality of this writing far exceeds my capabilities.

My dream began as a little desire to complete a small pamphlet outlining four scriptures and four steps to our Heavenly Father. But as I prayed, he revealed more scriptures, examples, and stories. He showed me how to make the ideas clearer, and he gave me the desire, strength, and ability to write this book. And so I share it with you, really, as our Father's book and not as my own. While I accept full responsibility for its errors and shortcomings, I give full credit to my Heavenly Father for any good things you may find within these pages.

I certainly want to thank my wife who has so patiently read each chapter more than once and who has so often encouraged me with ideas and inspiration to finish this book. I also thank my family members, many of whom have read all or parts of this manuscript and have given me important responses. Darla Isackson, my editor at Aspen Books, has been marvelously helpful. I deeply appreciate her wisdom and inspiration. I must also thank Paul Rawlins who copyedited the book and Jeanette Andrews who created the exquisite cover.

Lastly, I give a special thanks to those who graciously read this book in its early stages with all its mistakes and shortcomings and showed me how to make it better.

Dedication

Recently I gave a father's blessing to each of my children, and every blessing included strong admonitions to seek the Lord. Then I asked myself, "What greater gift could I give my children than the miracle of prayer, the miracle of speaking with their Heavenly Father, the Creator of the Universe?" Indeed, what greater gift could I give to anyone?

This book is dedicated to those persons who are sincerely seeking our Father in Heaven. If you are hoping to discover him in your prayers, then I have written this for you. My prayer is that this book will help you draw closer to the best Father of us all.

This book is also dedicated to my family. I started working seriously on this manuscript more than seven years ago, and I continued to write when I had no reason to believe it would ever be published. I did this for my wife and children, hoping that they would read it one day, even if no one else did. Within its pages I have tried to convey a vision of the miracle of prayer, a divine gift which I hope they will use effectively every day of their lives. I have labored because I love them. I want to say publicly to my wife, Peggy, and to my children, Alan, Keralyn, Justin, and Jarren, "I love you."

This book is written as a testimony of my personal convictions about prayer. I do not present these views as official LDS doctrine. They are entirely my own, but I sincerely believe what I have written here. I only hope that I am not misunderstood. That is my prayer.

Table of Contents

Introduction viii

"Chaplain, You'll Never Believe What Happened"
Chapter 1 1

God Is Your Father
Chapter 2 8

Approach Him Reverently
Chapter 3 17

Submit to Your Father First
Chapter 4 28

Request Specific Blessings in Faith
Chapter 5 56

Remembering Our Father's Son
Chapter 6 75

The Road to Faith in God
Chapter 7 87

The Blessings of Faith in God
Chapter 8 113

The Importance of Faith in God's Will
Chapter 9 144

Introduction

IHAVE BECOME AWARE WITH INCREASING CLARITY THAT HEAVENLY Father's greatest desire is to bless all of his children. Effective prayer is the key to accessing the help God is eager to extend to us. Because prayer is a conversation with God, our Heavenly Father, surely he would want to help us discover—from the scriptures, the experiences of others, and from our own experiences—some of the principles which underlie effective prayer.

Marital therapists often teach couples new ways of conversing with each other that help them understand each other better, show each other greater respect, and more accurately reveal each person's underlying feelings. If used faithfully, these effective "principles of communication" can draw a couple closer together.

Using the scriptures as our base, we can describe the most effective ways of conversing with God: spiritual "principles of prayer." These principles can draw us closer to him and help us understand him better. If we were closer to him, wouldn't we be happier? Wouldn't we be drawn more strongly into his miraculous world?

My own experiences have led me to believe that God's miracles (his divine intervention) fill the world around us. Our Father in Heaven loves to make miracles for those who turn to him with a sincere heart. The scriptures tell us that "the eyes of the Lord run to and fro throughout the whole earth, to shew himself strong in the behalf of them whose heart is perfect toward him" (2 Chr. 16:9).

In referring to the work and miracles which Christ did in our behalf, the apostle John said, "And there are also many other things which Jesus did, the which, if they should be written every one, I suppose that even the world itself could not contain the books that should be written" (John 21:25). How many miracles has Christ brought us since his resurrection? They are countless, and they are occurring every day to those with believing hearts.

Miracles are *natural* experiences, for we are really *spiritual* beings. Our essence is spiritual, and we wear our bodies like a garment. God is the Father of our spirits (Heb. 12:9), and we are his children. It is part of our spiritual heritage to commune with God and to participate in miraculous experiences with him. Joseph Smith said that it is the "first principle of the gospel . . . to know that we may converse with [God] as one man converses with another."[1] Heavenly Father created our world to train and develop our spiritual attributes. The apostle Peter said God's "divine power hath given unto us all things that pertain unto life and godliness . . . that by these [we] might be *partakers of the divine nature*" (2 Pet. 1:3–4; emphasis mine). Our challenge is to develop our spiritual selves, to transcend and control our physical selves.

If miracles are a part of our spiritual heritage, what then restricts our faith and blocks our spiritual development? I believe it is our tendency to set our hearts upon the physical things which we can see and hear, touch and taste or smell. One Gallup poll showed that Americans rank health, family, love, and friends ahead of God.[2] We could only do this because these things all appear more real to us than God does. Nevertheless, when we set our minds and hearts "so much upon the things of this world," our Heavenly Father says that the "Spirit of the Lord is grieved" and the "heavens withdraw themselves" (D&C 121:35, 37). Our Savior's kingdom, meanwhile, "is not of this world" (John 18:36). Although our world appears to be a physical one to us, it is not that way to God, who said, "all things unto me are spiritual" (D&C 29:34).

Marvelous possibilities open up to us when we drop our fixation with worldly things and exercise faith in God, the divine power in the universe, and in his principles. Jesus said, "He that believeth on me, the works that I do shall he do also; and greater works than these shall he do" (John 14:12). This is what our Heavenly Father wants us to learn.

Although the physical life is easier to see, only the spiritual life can deliver a lasting peace and happiness. One survey showed that people who are "highly spiritually committed" are far happier than the less spiritually committed.[3] I think this is so because spiritual growth and development is our deepest and most vital need. Only the spiritual life is full and abundant. That's why Christ came, that we "might have life, and . . . have it more abundantly" (John 10:10).

During my last years in college I had a number of miraculous experiences. After pondering them, I began to believe that how I had prayed had a lot to do with how God had responded. I took this conviction to the Third Marine Infantry Battalion at Camp Pendleton, California, where I served as a Navy chaplain. While there, I had an experience while counseling a young Baptist Marine that seemed to clarify some principles of prayer, both for the Marine and for myself. After we had prayed, using principles which Heavenly Father had revealed to us, this young Marine returned to my office the next week saying, "Chaplain, you'll never believe what happened."

I saw that the spiritual principles we had learned fit perfectly into a framework I had used as a missionary to teach investigators how to pray. So I used that framework to organize the ideas and began to share this Marine's story with a few others who seemed especially sincere, to help them to learn how to pray. Nearly all of those who learned these principles came back to report their own personal miracles. I hope this book will bring the same results for you.

Notes

1. Joseph Smith, *Teachings of the Prophet Joseph Smith*, comp. Joseph Fielding Smith (Salt Lake City: Deseret Book, 1976), 344–45; emphasis mine.
2. Gerry Avant, "Poll Studies Public View of the Savior," *Church News*, October 23, 1983, 4.
3. Ibid.

"Chaplain, You'll Never Believe What Happened"

IN THE SPRING OF 1983, I FINISHED MY MASTER'S DEGREE in counseling and was accepted into the Navy as an LDS chaplain. In July of 1983, the Navy sent me to their Chaplain's Basic Course in Newport, Rhode Island, and I graduated seven weeks later. My first assignment was with the 3rd Marine Infantry Battalion at Camp Pendleton, California. I soon learned that some Marines got into heartbreaking situations. One Friday during lunch, a young black Marine knocked at my office door. My afternoon was full and my lunch was half eaten. I wanted him to schedule a later appointment, but when I saw his ashen face with eyes like full moons, I let him in.

I asked how I could help, and he said, "Sir, I just came up positive for marijuana on this last drug test, and this is the second time. They're going to kick me out of the Corps."

I nodded, for I knew our battalion commander didn't tolerate drug use and always exacted the full penalty. That meant the loss of two months' pay, reduction in rank, confinement in the brig for at least sixty days, and a dishonorable discharge.

The corporal said, "I didn't do it. I smoked it that first time, but I learned my lesson. I've been clean ever since."

He then showed me a newspaper article that told about errors made in the system that occasionally convicted innocent Marines and sailors. He sounded sincere and was firm and quietly insistent. I thought he might be telling the truth. However, Marine officers considered drug test results to be conclusive evidence of drug use. To my knowledge, our commanding officer had discharged every Marine in our battalion who came up positive on a second drug test.

But this Marine's family was in trouble too, and he said, "Sir, I need to stay in the Marine Corps. I'm married to a woman who has five children from a previous marriage. We moved into base housing and still have barely enough money to pay our bills. Worse than that, my wife has bone cancer and is receiving radiation and chemotherapy at the base hospital. If I'm kicked out of the service, we'll never be able to afford her medical treatment."

I asked, "How can I help you?"

Corporal Johnson said, "I'm appearing before the company commander. Would you *please* come with me and say something in my behalf?"

He said he'd be summoned sometime that afternoon. That meant I'd have to cancel all my afternoon appointments, and I'd made important promises to other Marines. I thought I could help *them* but not him. He'd certainly get kicked out no matter what I said. And how could I know he was telling the truth? To speak inappropriately and be wrong would cost me credibility. Another Marine might genuinely need that credibility in the future.

Feeling helpless and humble, I began to pray in my heart, "Heavenly Father, what should I do? Is he telling me the truth?

What about his family? Should he stay in the Marines? How can I help him? What can I say to him?"

I prayed harder and listened for that still small voice whose spiritual impressions had become so important to me. After some time I heard Heavenly Father say, *I'm the only one who can help him now. Have him turn to the seventh chapter of Matthew and read verses seven through eleven.*

Before turning to the scripture I said, "Corporal Johnson, I can't help you. Your problem is too big for me, but God can help you. Listen to what he's saying."

Then we went to the Bible, and I felt inspiration flow into me as we read and discussed the verses. I felt I was understanding these words for the first time. Corporal Johnson's eyes widened as we both recognized how much our Heavenly Father loves us. Together we saw a real Father who is eager to help us. I continued to listen for promptings, and the Spirit said, *Have him stay in Matthew, turn to chapter six, and read verses five through eight.*

In this first part of the second scripture, we learned the requirement for using simple but honest words in prayer. When we finished reading and discussing it the Spirit said, *Now read verses nine through thirteen. This is the basic format I want him to use. It's not hard, just four simple steps.*

This was the Lord's Prayer, and we learned that Jesus gave much more guidance in it than I'd previously supposed. Through it we saw the Lord's four simple steps of prayer, and I discussed them as I was inspired by the Lord. Then the Spirit whispered, *Turn to James verses five through eight of the first chapter. Corporal Johnson has got to know what faith is about because I won't help him unless he has faith.*

So we read and discussed this third scripture, and when we finished, I heard, *This is the last scripture. Turn to the gospel of Mark, the ninth chapter, and read verses seventeen through twenty-nine. Some problems require more faith to resolve than others, and he needs to know how to get that extra faith.*

And so we read and discussed that fourth scripture together, and when we finished, I received a final prompting, *Pray with him.*

I asked Corporal Johnson if I could pray for him and he nodded his head. It was a simple prayer of perhaps a minute in length. I spoke just a few heartfelt sentences. Then I asked if he would pray. He hesitated, but the Spirit was there as he talked with God. His prayer was even shorter than mine, but very sincere, and when he finished, I asked, "Did you feel it? Did you feel the Spirit?"

He nodded yes. His eyes were misty and the fear had gone out of them. His whole body had relaxed. With a smile, he shook my hand and said, "I'm gonna be okay. I'll come back Monday and let you know what happened."

When I arrived for work Monday, I found a note taped on my door, asking me to contact him. My faith had slipped over the weekend and I groaned inside. I thought things hadn't gone well and that I would be asked to help him find a new home for his family. We were not able to meet on Monday. At noon on Tuesday, he knocked on my door and said, "Chaplain, you'll never believe what happened."

I tensed and waited for his explanation.

He said, "When I went into the commander's office, he asked me if I had anything to say, and I felt prompted to tell him my story exactly as I told it to you. When I finished, he was silent. He didn't say anything, but just looked at me for a long time.

"When he finally spoke, he said, 'I don't know whether to believe you or not, but I want to. You've been a good Marine, and I'm going to take a chance on you. I'll delay this paperwork, and we'll see if the battalion staff remembers to request it. If they forget, you're in luck.

"'Furthermore, I'm going to recommend you for Temporary

Additional Duty [a temporary assignment usually given as a reward] with another unit. I'll date it prior to the time we were notified of your drug test. If the transfer is approved, personnel will take your name off the battalion rolls. There's a good chance battalion personnel might forget about you.

"'As I said, I want to believe you. If we hear nothing from the battalion, you're in the clear. On the other hand, if you ever test positive for drugs again, I'll bring my full authority against you.'"

After a pause Corporal Johnson added, "Then he tore up the charges, right in front of my eyes."

He continued, "I had been praying that whole afternoon while I was waiting to see my commanding officer. Now I *know* God hears and answers prayers."

After he left, I made a mental note to check the battalion legal officer's board for pending disciplinary action. It was a grease-board that listed every Marine confined to the brig. It also listed every pending dishonorable discharge. I checked it routinely every day because I visited our Marines in the brig and the correctional custody facility. Corporal Johnson's name never appeared on the board.

Later Corporal Johnson told me that his temporary transfer came through and personnel would be taking his name off our battalion rolls. That was a great blessing for him because he never returned to the battalion. Heavenly Father enabled him to stay home with his family and sick wife while our unit deployed on our six-month cruise in the Pacific.

I wrote down the four scriptures that had made such a difference to Corporal Johnson and made notes on my understanding of the four steps revealed to us. Whenever a Marine presented me with a tough situation, I would tell him Corporal Johnson's story and ask if he wanted to see these scriptures. Following a session, I would often hear, "I never understood that before."

These are the notes I kept from my session with Corporal Johnson, hoping to share the experience with others. These notes led me to a lifetime study that eventually became this book.

The First Scripture
God is your Father who loves you and gives you good things. (Matt. 7:7–11)

The Second Scripture
Have a simple, heart-to-heart talk with your Heavenly Father. (Matt. 6:5–8)

Four Simple Steps to Our Father (Matt. 6:9–13)
Lord Teach Us to Pray (Luke 11:1)

Step One—Our Heavenly Father
Hallowed Be Thy Name (Matt. 6:9)

- Approach God with reverence and respect.
- Descend into the depths of humility.

Step Two—I thank thee
Thy Will Be Done (Matt. 6:10)

- Submit to your Father first.
- Big mistake #1 is to skip this step.
- Thank your Father sincerely for each blessing.
- Pause and praise before you weep and wail.
- Listen for God's will, which is your divine homework.
- Inventory and confess each of your sins.
- Do your homework. Repent! Obey the commandments.

Step Three—I ask thee
Give Us This Day Our Daily Bread. (Matt. 6:11–13)

- Now you can focus on your own righteous desires.
- Big mistake #2 is to make an unrighteous request.

Step Four—In the name of Jesus Christ. Amen.

The Third Scripture

Ask in faith, nothing wavering. (James 1:5–7)

- Big mistake #3 is to waver in our faith.
- We waver because we don't know the Lord's will.

The Fourth Scripture

Help thou mine unbelief. (Mark 9:17–29)

- You can ask for faith.

By nothing, but by prayer and fasting.

- Fasting is doing without food and water for 24 hours.
- Begin, continue, and end the fast with prayer.

2

God Is Your Father

The First Scripture

The first scripture I was inspired to read with Corporal Johnson was one we are all familiar with.

> *Ask, and it shall be given you; seek, and ye shall find; knock, and it shall be opened unto you:*
>
> *For every one that asketh receiveth; and he that seeketh findeth; and to him that knocketh it shall be opened.*
>
> *Or what man is there of you, whom if his son ask bread, will he give him a stone?*
>
> *Or if he ask a fish, will he give him a serpent?*
>
> *If ye then, being evil, know how to give good gifts unto your children, how much more shall your Father which is in heaven give good things to them that ask him? (Matt. 7:7–11)*[1]

Notice how the Lord uses the word *shall,* as opposed to the words *might* or *perhaps.*

It *shall* be given you.

Ye *shall* find.

It *shall* be opened unto you.

Jesus emphasized this idea with a concrete example about fathers. If your son asked for bread, would you give him a stone? If your daughter asked for dinner, would you give her a snake? We don't give stones or snakes to our children when they ask for food. We give them food and clothing because it is part of our divine nature. Building upon these examples, the Savior drove home his point: "If ye then, being evil, know how to give good gifts unto your children, *how much more* shall your Father which is in heaven give good things to them that ask him?" (Matt. 7:11; emphasis mine).

How much more does your Heavenly Father love you than does your own earthly father? How much more will he help fill your genuine needs? How much more can you count on him to be there when you need him? How much more will he feel the pain you are feeling? How much more does he care about you than any father on earth does?

Your Heavenly Father is anxious to help you! His eyes "run to and fro throughout the whole earth, to shew himself strong in the behalf of them whose heart is perfect toward him" (2 Chr. 16:9). Can you believe he is deeply committed to your welfare? If you can believe this, you can have blessings unmeasured. It's easy to trust someone when you know they love you, and your faith will grow each time you sense God's love and caring.

Even in his suffering, Christ knew our Father loved him. In the Garden of Gethsemane, he submitted himself utterly to God. When his suffering was so great "and his sweat was as it were great drops of blood falling down to the ground" (Luke 22:44), he cried out, "O my Father . . . let this cup pass from me: nevertheless not as I will, but as thou wilt" (Matt. 26:39). Later, as he hung on the cross, he implored, "My God, my God, why hast thou forsaken me?" (Matt. 27:46). Yet after his crucifixion, he appeared to Mary at the tomb and affirmed his commitment to the Father, saying, "I ascend unto my Father, and your Father; and to my God, and your God" (John 20:17).

The God of heaven and earth is our Father. Christ called him *Abba,*[2] which in Hebrew is "a personal, familial term for father."[3] Our English equivalent would be something like *dad* or *daddy.*[4] But *Abba* wasn't reserved exclusively for our Savior's use. Paul suggested that because the Spirit bears witness that we are the children of God, we too can cry, "Abba, Father" (Rom. 8:15). John records the Savior or his disciples referring to God as "Father" 114 times.[5] This is their testimony of our Father's love for each of us. Can you feel it? Can you see his vital interest in your thoughts, your feelings, and your life?

The King's Law

A general in the U.S. Air Force on a visit to Morocco was taken on a tour into the Moroccan countryside. As his car approached the top of a hill he saw that the limousine ahead had pulled off the road. An old shepherd was talking to the driver of the parked limousine while a flock of fifteen or twenty sheep waited nearby. There had been an accident, and the king's driver had hit one of the old shepherd's lambs. Under the king's law, the old shepherd was now entitled to the value of a hundred mature sheep, but the same law required the lamb to be slain and the meat shared among the people. The general's interpreter commented, "The old shepherd will not accept the money . . . because of the love he has for each of his sheep. They never do."

Then the general noticed the "old shepherd reach down, lift the injured lamb in his arms, and place it in a large pouch on the front of his robe. He kept stroking its head, repeating the same word over and over again." When the general asked what the word meant he was told, "Oh, he is calling it by name. All of his sheep have a name, for he is their shepherd, and the good shepherds know each one of their sheep by name."⁶

The old shepherd refused the king's offer and quietly led his flock back into the desert with the injured lamb tucked safely in his pouch.

Christ has said, "I am the good shepherd, and know my sheep . . . and I lay down my life for the sheep" (John 10:14–15). How much does our Heavenly Father love us to sacrifice his only Son, the Lamb of God? How deeply can you believe in this love?

If you want a miracle, you must believe our Heavenly Father loves you. This is the first step to a vibrant faith. To believe otherwise doesn't allow a close relationship with God. Who can trust in God while believing that he might be uncaring or even unkind? Such a mindset will restrain our faith.

Think again of the old shepherd who could have increased his flock sixfold. He passed up the financial opportunity of a lifetime, cradled the little lamb to his breast, stroked its head tenderly, and gently called its name. The money was nothing to him compared to the life of his little lamb.

So it is with our Father, who calls us his "little flock" (D&C 6:34). He is our Heavenly Shepherd and we are his little lambs. He knows you intimately and is gently calling your name. He loves you dearly and would enfold you warmly in his arms. Can you understand how much he cares? Can you imagine him holding you tenderly?

When you realize how much God loves you, then you can draw near to him and he can draw near to you (Zech. 1:3; James 4:8; Rev. 3:20). You are completely free. The first move is yours, but it is so much easier when you know he deeply cares. When you sense how much more he loves you than the old shepherd loved the lamb, *then* you can believe he will answer your righteous prayer.

Good Things

Our Savior said, "Whatsoever thing ye shall ask the Father in my name, *which is good,* in faith believing that ye shall receive, behold, it shall be done unto you" (Moro. 7:26; emphasis mine). So what are the good things God says he will give us? We can rest assured that God will never give us sinful or immoral things. We may get them on our own, but he will never give them to us. For example, God would never grant us revenge, because he commands us to forgive. Pause for a moment and ask yourself whether a good father would want for his children:

- A pretentious palace or a happy home?
- A calculated career or meaningful work?
- An easy existence or transcending strength?
- Permission to sin or wisdom to obey?
- An elegant auto or trustworthy transportation?
- A trendy lifestyle or a satisfying life?

The answers are a key to understanding God. What does *he* think is good? If we can learn this, we can come to understand which requests he might or might not grant. All fathers who love their children evaluate each request to determine the potential harm or good to their child. They have their eye on their child's ultimate development and care about what their children become. Loving parents want their children to reach worthy goals, and they also care deeply about their children's charity, integrity, courage, etc.

Our Father certainly cares about our faith in him and considers which gifts will develop this quality. He cares even more about our compassion for others. The apostle Paul said that if we don't have charity, we are nothing (1 Cor. 13). So we need to ask ourselves, What if God granted my request? Would it foster my generosity or my selfishness? Would it increase my wisdom? If I receive my request, will I be more or less valuable in service to others? Could it harden my heart? Would it help me to remember him? Would it spoil me?

Would God Spoil Us?

The word *spoil* means "to damage or injure in such a way as to make useless, [or] valueless, etc."[7] Perhaps the greatest question a parent should ask before granting a request is this: "Will it spoil the child?"

I remember the story of a rich woman who registered in a lavish hotel. Servants followed her, pushing her son along in a wheelchair. Since his leg muscles were not atrophied, a guest asked what caused her son's paralysis. She replied, "Oh, he can walk, but thank God he doesn't have to."

Has this mother built her son's confidence? Has she expanded his initiative? Consider the ugliness of his assenting uselessness. Consider the damage to his soul and self-esteem. Consider how she has diminished his sense of contribution to the people around him. Could he really feel good about himself, knowing he is doing nothing useful or helpful for anyone else?

We spoil children if we grant every selfish wish or protect them from every disappointment and challenge. We cripple their growth if we gratify their every appetite and feed them when they are full. It is indulgence that leads us to entertain them rather than teach them. When we carry children who should walk, we eliminate their frustration for the moment, but we diminish their long-range possibilities. Indulgence sacrifices character for pleasure. I saw a television documentary in August 1989 on drug use. Teenage addicts, sitting on a stone wall, told the reporters they had been given drugs by their addicted parents. No caring father in his right mind could destroy a child in that way, and it would be unthinkable for God to grant anything which would encourage us to become useless or greedy or selfish or to destroy any part of our potential. Such giving could only replace the beauty of a soul with ugliness. What beauty is manifested in a spoiled child's pouting?

Each of us in our human condition must wrestle with some degree of greed or selfishness, and God will not indulge us and spoil our character. We may resent his refusal to indulge us when we make unwise requests, but he always acts in our best interest, according to his higher knowledge.

Our Father knows that withholding or delaying gifts can sometimes strengthen us. A farmer once explained to a visitor to his orchard, "These trees could go without rain for another two weeks. . . . When they were young, I frequently kept water from them. This hardship caused them to send their roots deeper into the soil in search of moisture. Now mine are the deepest rooted trees in the area. While others are being scorched by the sun, these are finding moisture at greater depth."[8] Another farmer told his daughter to withhold water from corn plants because too much water would cause them to grow so fast they would topple over. Their roots would not support their height.[9]

Bill Sands was an ex-convict who served time in solitary confinement in San Quentin prison for armed robbery. When he was released on parole he worked successfully in many different careers, one of which was show business. Eventually though, he was led to set up a program to help ex-convicts live responsibly in their communities. He called it The Seventh Step. Local businessmen volunteered to sponsor individual convicts by helping them find jobs and adjust to life outside of prison. Some sponsors were wiser than others.

One well-meaning businessman sponsored a convict named Johnny Brand. The sponsor invited the convict to live in his home, got him into the country club, and bought him expensive clothing, etc. The result of all this was that the convict began drinking, turning down job offers, and believing he had a right to a lavish, hassle-free lifestyle. The sponsor's indulgence actually helped the convict become dependent and irresponsible. Program leaders stopped the sponsor just in time to prevent Johnny's failure.[10] This is why God won't always say yes to our requests. He must evaluate whether granting a request will be good for our growth and development.

I want my children to learn to love others, to become self-disciplined and patient. A child who fails to acquire love and patience could become an abusive parent. But patience can only be developed in frustrating circumstances, and love is developed by learning to set aside our own interests. A child acquires self-discipline by making demands of himself, not by making demands of others. Sometimes a thing must be withheld to promote our growth. C.S. Lewis said, "We are . . . in very truth, a Divine work of art, something that God is making, and therefore something with which He will not be satisfied until it has a certain character."[11] Thus we can see that our Heavenly Father might withhold some things because he is trying to perfect our character.

Does all this mean that God won't give us anything? No, of course not. President Marion G. Romney has said that "there seems to be no limitation as to when, where, and what we should pray about."[12] However, we do need to learn the difference between our real needs and our mere wants. As we learn to recognize our Father's best gifts and as we cultivate our desire to seek them, we will grow spiritually and our prayers will become more effective. As a father, I work hard to provide for my children, and I try to grant every reasonable request. In one way or another, I ensure that my children have everything they really need. Our Heavenly Father is infinitely more loving than I am, and he is always available to us. He will work countless miracles to meet our genuine needs. God is our Father who loves us and gives us every *good* thing.

Notes

1. For a more meaningful experience, read the verses from the Bible and ask Heavenly Father to help you understand them. Christ said, "Therefore, go ye unto your homes, and ponder upon the things which I have said, and ask of the Father, in my name, that ye may understand" (3 Ne. 17:3).
2. Mark 14:36.
3. Bible Dictionary, Holy Bible, LDS Version, 600.
4. See David B. Guralnik, ed., *Webster's New World Dictionary of the American Language,* 2nd college ed. (Cleveland: William Collins & World Publishing Co., Inc., 1974), 505, for the terms *familial* and *familiar,* etc.
5. Robert Young, *Young's Analytical Concordance to the Bible* (Grand Rapids, Michigan: Eerdman's Publishing Company, 1975), 333–34.
6. John R. Lasater, "Shepherds of Israel," *Ensign,* May 1988, 74.
7. *Webster's New World Dictionary*, 1375.
8. Dennis J. De Haan, "Deep Roots," *Our Daily Bread,* March-May 1986, April 5.
9. Sandra Stallings, "A Lesson in the Corn Patch," *New Era,* July 1986, 13.
10. Bill Sands, *The Seventh Step* (New York: The New American Library, Inc., 1967), 128.
11. C.S. Lewis, *The Problem of Pain* (New York: Macmillan Publishing Co., Inc., 1978), 42.
12. Marion G. Romney, "Prayer Is the Key," *Ensign,* January 1976, 4.

3

Approach Him Reverently

The Second Scripture

And when thou prayest, thou shalt not be as the hypocrites are: for they love to pray standing in the synagogues and in the corners of the streets, that they may be seen of men. Verily I say unto you, They have their reward.

But thou, when thou prayest, enter into thy closet, and when thou hast shut thy door, pray to thy Father which is in secret; and thy Father which seeth in secret shall reward thee openly.

But when ye pray, use not vain repetitions, as the heathen do: for they think that they shall be heard for their much speaking.

Be not ye therefore like unto them: for your Father knoweth what things ye have need of, before ye ask him. (Matt. 6:5–8)

Prayers are generally private matters between us and our Father. They're honest and simple conversations with a wonderful "Counsellor" (Isa. 9:6). They are not pretentious displays, but are instead real talks with a real Father. Vain repetitions can indicate doubt that we've been heard, or they can reveal a prideful desire to "appear" righteous. In neither case could we honestly expect a miraculous answer. Doubt isn't faith. Faith is something more than words, and it is a vital forerunner to miracles: "For if there be no faith among the children of men God can do no miracle among them; wherefore, he showed not himself until after their faith" (Ether 12:12).

We can easily imagine that pretending to be righteous is no more pleasing to God than doubting him. Thus, vain repetitions won't bring miracles. However it is the "vain" we need to worry about and not the repetitions. Sincere repetitions of righteous requests are encouraged. Think of the parable of the importunate widow whose request was finally granted.

"Vain" may be interpreted as prideful or self-serving. Repetitions of prideful requests could never be pleasing and would rarely lead to having the request granted.

The Second Scripture Continued

The next verses are *The Lord's Prayer*. Jesus gave this prayer pattern in response to a request from one of his disciples, who said, "Lord, teach us to pray" (Luke 11:1). Jesus said, "After this manner therefore pray ye" (Matt. 6:9). You can see that his prayer is an example (within which we find four steps) for structuring our own conversations with our Father in Heaven.

> *Our Father which art in heaven, Hallowed be thy name.*
> *Thy kingdom come. Thy will be done in earth, as it is in heaven.*
> *Give us this day our daily bread.*
> *And forgive us our debts, as we forgive our debtors.*
> *And lead us not into temptation, but deliver us from evil:*
> *For thine is the kingdom, and the power, and the glory, for ever.*
> *Amen. (Matt. 6:9–13)*

Step One
Our Father which art in heaven

Jesus begins by humbly addressing his Father. He doesn't just begin talking. How would you ask for a serious conversation with a potential benefactor? Wouldn't you begin by respectfully addressing him or her by name? For example, if I wanted to speak seriously with someone named Jim, I'd say with genuine respect, "Jim, may I talk with you?" That would be more polite, more courteous, and more considerate of his feelings than just blurting out my story. Doesn't our Father deserve our best manners? The opportunity to talk with God is an even greater privilege than talking to a friend you can really trust. And since he's there as a serious counselor, we should prepare ourselves for each therapeutic session.

When speaking with God, it is only wisdom to do as Christ taught. Go to a secret closet, kneel in reverence, and request a special audience with God. Approach him as you would approach the throne of a king. Don't forget that he rules the universe. Notice how humble, reverent, and considerate Christ is of his Father's feelings when he utters: "Our Father which art in heaven, Hallowed be thy name" (Matt. 6:9).

Hallowed

Something hallowed has been "made holy or sacred" or is "honored as holy; [or] venerated." To hallow is to honor and give "high regard or great respect." It means to "treat with deference and courtesy." To venerate our Heavenly Father would mean to worship, reverence, and love him.[1] It is evident that Christ revered his Father and that this was an important mark of their relationship. When Moses approached God at the burning bush, he was told, "Draw not nigh hither: put off thy shoes from off thy feet, for the place whereon thou standest is holy ground" (Ex. 3:5). His compliance showed his respect.

Reverence is attractive to the Lord, but irreverence or rudeness, in any of their forms, is repulsive. Recently, my little two-year-old son tugged on my pants and demanded, "Gimme juice!"

I said, "No."

"Gimme juice!" he insisted.

I repeated, "No."

This continued until he softened. Then I said gently, "Say please."

"Please?" he ventured.

When he became more respectful (which is another way of saying he became more reverent), I gave him some juice. His little *please* was far more appealing than his rude manner.

Your reverence must be sincere. Some folks start out with an appealing *please*, but it's a ruse they soon drop if you politely refuse them. Their courtesy quickly changes to manipulations and demands.

Chaim Potok told of some beggars in Macao whose manner was far from reverent. A chaplain, Arthur Leiden, went to Macao on leave from Korea with a friend, Gershon Loran. Their guide warned them against giving anything to the beggars in the temple, but Arthur ignored the warning and gave one a coin. Immediately he was inundated with angry beggars *demanding* money from him. They pressed around to hold him tight while waving threatening canes and sticks. The chaplain was shaken, but he didn't give them any more coins. He waited until the guide and his friend arrived to free him from the crowd. The beggars certainly weren't reverent.[2] The irony is that none of them received anything more from Arthur except ill will.

God won't respond to rude requests. How would you have responded to the demands of the beggars of Macao? If you had known what would happen, would you have given them anything? Would you judge them as ungrateful or manipulative? Would their actions offend you? Would you be inclined to joyously grant their requests? On the other hand, how would you respond to a humble "Please?"

As it is with our fellowmen, so it is with our Heavenly Father, who is perfect in his respect toward us and who rightly expects respect in return. A little respect goes a long way, and a lot of respect goes farther. Are you being or have you been unwittingly discourteous in your manner of prayer? Have you ever pouted or sulked if your request wasn't granted? Do you need to examine your manners with God?

Humility and Reverence

Look at the prodigal son's approach to his father when he returned home for help. The scriptures record that "when he came to himself, he said, How many hired servants of my father's have bread enough and to spare, and I perish with hunger! I will arise and go to my father, and will say unto him, Father, I have sinned against heaven, and before thee, And am no more worthy to be called thy son: make me as one of thy hired servants" (Luke 15:17–19).

Notice his humility and reverence. What a contrast with the beggars of Macao. Notice how he was humbled and prepared to receive whatever his father might offer. His highest hope was to work as a servant for his dad. Ironically, his humble return to his father resulted in a gift and celebration far greater than that which would be given for a servant, for his father received him as his son. Similarly, we will be received as God's children when we humble ourselves before him.

Humility in prayer indicates that we understand the differences between ourselves and God, who has said, "For my thoughts are not your thoughts, neither are your ways my ways, saith the LORD. For as the heavens are higher than the earth, so are my ways higher than your ways, and my thoughts than your thoughts" (Isa. 55:8–9). He wants to know if we can see the truth about ourselves. Someone who can't recognize this simple truth can't be humble.

Christ said, "Ye are my friends, if ye do whatsoever I command you" (John 15:14). He requires our respect and obedience if we want his help. He set it up that way to interrupt our selfish focus and help us see beyond our little world. When we want to close the distance between us, we have to seek him on *his* terms, which are that we be honest and wise enough to recognize our low station. Real understanding of God and ourselves creates humility and reverence in his presence.

Real reverence reaches Heavenly Father in a real way. Even the vilest of sinners can obtain good things from God if they approach him humbly. Manasseh was a loathsome king of Judah who built altars to false gods and groves for licentious worship practices. He burned some of his children alive as sacrifices to his false gods. He listened to astrologers "and used enchantments, and used witchcraft, and dealt with a familiar spirit, and with wizards: he wrought much evil in the sight of the LORD, to provoke him to anger. And he set a carved image, the idol which he had made, in the house of God" (2 Chr. 33:6–7).

So God brought in the Assyrians, who took Manasseh[3] captive to Assyria in chains. Then Manasseh "besought the LORD his God, and *humbled himself greatly* before the God of his fathers, And prayed unto him: and [God] was intreated of him, and heard his supplication, and brought him again to Jerusalem into his kingdom. Then Manasseh knew that the LORD he was God" (2 Chr. 33:10–13; emphasis mine).

The prophet Daniel had an extraordinary relationship with God and received many miraculous blessings and gifts from him. But Daniel did not approach his Father carelessly. Instead he approached God with deep respect and humility. We can see his marvelous humility by studying one of his prayers. He said, "And I set my face unto the Lord God, to seek by prayer and supplications, with fasting, and sackcloth, and ashes: And I prayed unto the LORD my God, and made my confession" (Dan. 9:3–4).

To get an idea of the pains Daniel took to humble himself, we can go to the dictionaries. Supplications are humble petitions.[4] Fasting means to "abstain from all or some kinds of food as a . . . sign of mourning."[5] Sackcloth is "a dark-colored material of goat or camel hair used for making grain bags and garments. . . . A garment of sackcloth was uncomfortable and was therefore worn by those in mourning . . . [as] a sign of distress and repentance."[6] "Ashes signify destruction . . . and are contrasted with glory. Sitting on them or putting them on one's head were rituals of mourning and repentance. . . . Ashes are also mentioned as symbolic of insignificance."[7] Confession is "a general acknowledgement of sin."[8]

Daniel devotes this entire chapter to humbling himself before our Father, and at the end of his confession, the angel Gabriel comes to give him "skill and understanding" (Dan. 9:22). In the next chapter, Daniel humbles himself again for three weeks, and another angel comes to answer his prayer and says: "From the first day that thou didst . . . chasten thyself before thy God, thy words were heard, and I am come for thy words" (Dan. 10:12).

The word *chasten* means "to punish in order to correct or make better; chastise . . . subdue . . . to make purer in style; [or] refine."[9] So after Daniel chastises, or humbles, himself, he is visited by two angels, both of whom commented that Daniel was "greatly beloved" (Dan. 9:23; 10:11). Can the connection between humility and God's affection be more clear? The Lord told King Josiah, "Because thine heart was tender, and thou didst humble thyself before [me] . . . I have even heard thee also saith the Lord" (2 Chr. 34:27).

President David O. McKay said "humility is the solid foundation of all the virtues."[10] We know that it is an essential ingredient of charity (1 Cor. 13:4–6). A careful search of the scriptures will show that the Lord "resisteth the proud, and giveth grace to the humble" (1 Pet. 5:5). A quick review of various concordances under the key word *humility* and its synonyms (humble, penitent, meek, contrite, mild, submissive, subjection, resignation, self-abasement, mortification, etc.) will reveal many more scriptures extolling humility before God.

Pharaoh refused to humble himself before the Lord, so God gave him and the Egyptians lessons on humility with the ten plagues (see Ex. 10:3–4). Our Heavenly Father took the Israelites into the wilderness to humble them. Moses couldn't have been more clear when he told them to "remember all the way which the LORD thy God led thee these forty years in the wilderness, to humble thee" (Deut. 8:2).

The Lord emphasized the importance of humility to King Solomon at the temple dedication by saying: "If my people, which are called by my name, shall humble themselves, and pray, and seek my face, and turn from their wicked ways; then will I hear from heaven, and will forgive their sin, and will heal their land" (2 Chr. 7:14). He told Isaiah, "I dwell in the high and holy place, with him also that is of a contrite and humble spirit, to revive the spirit of the humble, and to revive the heart of the contrite ones" (Isa. 57:15). When one is contrite, one is "feeling deep sorrow or remorse for having sinned or done wrong; penitent."[11] Jesus himself spoke plainly, saying, "And whosoever shall exalt himself shall be abased; and he that shall humble himself shall be exalted" (Matt. 23:12).

Although the sacrifices of the Law of Moses are no longer required, the Lord still requires the sacrifice of a broken heart and a contrite spirit (Ps. 51:17). Proud men crowd God out of their hearts, minds, and lives because they are too concerned about their own affairs. Humility fosters the sacrifice of selfish concerns and brings men closer to God.

Humility is crucial to revelation and to miracles. All of the prophets were humble before God. The Jews regard Moses as the greatest of all their prophets. He was their lawgiver who delivered them from Egypt and established them as a nation. Moses' humility was heightened after he saw God's creations. Afterward he collapsed and said, "Now, for this cause I know that man is nothing, which thing I never had supposed" (Moses 1:10). Our Heavenly Father worked so many miracles through Moses, at least in part, because he was "very meek, above all the men which were upon the face of the earth" (Num. 12:3). As we shall see in chapter five, faith is a vital ingredient in any miracle, and humility is vital to faith. Moroni said we "cannot have faith and hope, save [we] shall be meek, and lowly of heart" (Moro. 7:43). So Moses' great humility was a necessary part of his great faith.

Many of the prophets professed their humility explicitly in the scriptures. Abraham confessed to God, "I . . . am but dust and ashes" (Gen. 18:27). Ammon said, "I know that I am nothing; . . . I am weak" (Alma 26:12). A Book of Mormon prophet who saw the big picture said, "O how great is the nothingness of the children of men . . . less than the dust of the earth" (Hel. 12:7). Samuel the prophet reminded Saul, "When thou wast little in thine own sight . . . the LORD anointed thee king over Israel" (1 Sam. 15:16–17). King Solomon asked for wisdom because he was very humble. He told God, "I am but a little child: I know not how to go out or come in. . . . And the speech pleased the Lord" (1 Kgs. 3:7–10). Our Lord Jesus said, "Take my yoke upon you, and learn of me; for I am meek and lowly in heart: and ye shall find rest unto your souls" (Matt. 11:29).

Many persons wonder why they seem unable to hear the still

small voice of the Holy Spirit. Could it be that the problem is pride? Nephi said the proud "are they whom [God] despiseth; and save they shall cast these things [pride] away, and consider themselves fools before God, and come down in the depths of humility, he will not open unto them" (2 Ne. 9:42).

Why are so many miracles received during times of crushing crisis? Because we are so humbled? Does God allow suffering to humble us? Do we need such extreme circumstances to pulverize our pride so God can bless us? Are we ordinarily too proud to search the scriptures or pray sincerely or honestly face our sins?

Alma entreated everyone: "Let your sins trouble you, with that trouble which shall bring you down unto repentance. . . . Do not endeavor to excuse yourself in the least point because of your sins, by denying the justice of God; but do you let the justice of God, and his mercy, and his long-suffering have full sway in your heart; and let it bring you down to the dust in humility (Alma 42:29–30). Honestly facing our sins will bring us down to the depths of humility. Prophets, sacrificing food and pleasures, have gone into the desert to obtain a proper and humbling perspective of God. They've faced their sins and realized their own nothingness. Only then did they meet our Heavenly Father.

Humility before God is a significant part of the respect necessary for a successful relationship with God. Actually, respect is the foundation of all successful relationships. What happens to the relationship of a married couple when one spouse loses all respect for the other? What happens to their communication? What happens to their love, trust, and faith in each other? Is it really possible to have love without respect?

Yet we manifest disrespect if we approach the Lord in an attitude of carelessness or indifference. Jesus drove the money changers out of the temple because in their casual, "business as usual" attitude he saw no respect for his Father in Heaven.

Alma asked, "Behold, are ye stripped of pride? I say unto you, if ye are not ye are not prepared to meet God" (Alma 5:28). King Benjamin implored us to "always retain in remembrance, the greatness of God, and your own nothingness, . . . and humble yourselves even in the depths of humility, calling on the name of the Lord daily" (Mosiah 4:11). And as Thomas B. Marsh learned, "Be thou humble; and the Lord thy God shall lead thee by the hand, and give thee answer to thy prayers" (D&C 112:10).

So the first step toward pulling the powers of heaven into our lives is to call to our Heavenly Father with reverence and respect, descending into the depths of humility before him.

Notes

1. David B. Guralnik, ed., *Webster's New World Dictionary of the American Language,* 2nd college ed. (Cleveland: William Collins & World Publishing Co., Inc., 1974), 631.
2. Chaim Potok, *The Book of Lights* (New York: Fawcett Crest, 1981), 314–17.
3. Verse 11 says that "the Lord brought upon them the captains of the host of the king of Assyria, which took Manasseh." It looks to me as though the Lord actively intervened in this instance, while letting the Assyrians operate.
4. J. B. Sykes, ed., *The Concise Oxford Dictionary of Current English* (Oxford: Oxford University Press, 1976), 1160.
5. Ibid., 378.
6. Paul J. Achtemeier, general ed., *Harper's Bible Dictionary* (San Francisco: Harper & Row, Publishers, 1985), 890.
7. Ibid., 75.
8. *Webster's New World Dictionary,* 297.
9. Ibid., 241.
10. David O. McKay. In Obert C. Tanner, *Christ's Ideals for Living* (Salt Lake City: Obert C. and Grace A. Tanner Foundation, 1981), 39.
11. *Webster's New World Dictionary,* 309; emphasis mine.

4

Submit to Your Father First

The Second Scripture Continued

> *Thy kingdom come. Thy will be done in earth, as it is in heaven. (Matt. 6:10)*

Step Two

Did you notice how Jesus immediately shows his submissiveness to our Father? He does this before saying anything else. Does he understand something that many of us don't understand? The importance of submitting to our Heavenly Father is given the highest priority in scripture. The apostle James says it clearly: "Submit yourselves therefore to God" (James 4:7). On two separate occasions, Alma urges everyone to become submissive unto God (Alma 7:23 and 13:28). King Benjamin adds some details, saying, "For the natural man is an enemy to God, and has been from the fall of Adam, and will be, forever and ever, *unless he yields* to the enticings of the Holy Spirit . . . and becometh as a child, *submissive, . . . willing to submit* to all things which the Lord seeth fit to inflict upon him, *even as a child doth submit* to his father" (Mosiah 3:19; emphasis mine).

How often is this most important act hindered by our pride or selfishness? Leaping to our own concerns might be the single biggest mistake most of us make in prayer. We're so possessed by our own desires that we ignore the desires of our Heavenly Father. And yet there are two great ironies about this failure.

The first is that our Father wants to give us the very best things in life. Nephi said that our Heavenly Father is utterly selfless in his pursuit of our best interests, that "he doeth not anything save it be for the benefit of the world; for he loveth the world" (2 Ne. 26:24). Think again of the old shepherd in the previous chapter who refused to sacrifice his lamb to increase his flock. Imagine that you are God's lamb whom he lifts into the warmth of his pouch, calling you by name and carrying you away to dress your wounds and nurture your soul. He loves you more than the old shepherd loved his lamb.

The second irony is that he alone *knows* what is best for us because of his infinite, higher point of view. So often, we reap misery or unhappiness simply because we fail to seek or heed our Heavenly Father's counsel. A pilot learned the value of a higher point of view while flying a small plane over a two-lane highway near Hiram, Ohio. High in the air, he saw a lone blue car ascend one side of a hill and a convoy of cars start up the other side. He saw the rear car in the convoy pull out to pass, a course which would cause it to crash head-on into the lone blue car approaching the top of the hill from the opposite direction. He tried frantically to warn each driver, but failed, and later learned that all six persons involved in the crash had died.

Later, on the ground while tying down his plane, he was still shaking when a thought came into his mind: "'Now you know how our Heavenly Father feels as he must sit, . . . [and] watch while we ignore his spiritual pleadings.'"[1] Our Heavenly Father knows what is coming down the road to meet us. He knows what is in our best long-term interest, and he wants what will make us happiest. With this in mind, does it make sense to ignore his desires or refuse to submit to his counsel?

To *submit* means to "yield oneself to the authority or will of another."[2] In prayer, it means to yield to God's authority and will. To *yield* means "to give or render . . . [whatever is] fitting, right-fully owed, or required."[3] Thus, when Jesus tells us to "render therefore unto Caesar the things which are Caesar's" he simply means that we are to submit to governmental authority as well as to God's will.

To *submit* also means "to give up and cease resistance or contention."[4] In other words, in order to submit to God, we have to stop resisting him and willingly render to him whatever he requires of us. It is the opposite of rebellion, and rebellion must be dropped if we want to receive help from heaven.

Submission clearly is related to the humility we discussed in the previous chapter, but goes beyond it because a person can *resist,* even *rebel against* another in a most humble way.

Dr. Neil Flinders said in one of his classes at BYU that we must submit to God each day. He said that "submission to God is *not* the same thing as commitment to him. Submission is greater than commitment. Submission is to surrender one's will to him, and then he will direct our lives for good. Both submission and commitment can be measured by activity in church, but ultimate happiness, personal peace and spiritual fulfillment will attend only submission."[5] We can be active in church and committed to God but still not feel his Spirit in prayer if we are not submissive to his will.

Our Savior testifies of the peace and fulfillment which attend submission. He says, "Come unto me, all ye that labour and are heavy laden, and I will give you rest. Take my yoke upon you, and learn of me; for I am meek and lowly in heart; and ye shall find rest unto your souls" (Matt. 11:28–29). The yoke is "a wooden bar or frame by which two draft animals (such as oxen) are joined at the heads or necks for working together."[6] As such, it is a symbol of the oxen's submission to the will of the master, of accepting whatever burdens or tasks the master might impose.

The blessing that accompanies submission to Christ is that we link ourselves to him. Sometimes we refer to the "yoke of marriage," meaning that we tie or bind our lives and our destinies with that of our companions. When we submit to God by taking the yoke of Christ upon us, he becomes our partner in the harness. When we take Christ's yoke upon us, we bring his power into our lives and our burdens become light. We find rest unto our souls only when we accept Christ's yoke.

In my own personal prayers, when I am not submissive, I do not feel the Spirit. Helaman described a congregation whose fasting, prayer, and worship effectively purified and sanctified the people's hearts "because of . . . yielding their hearts unto God" (Hel. 3:35). I believe this cleansing, purifying, and sanctifying occurs when we feel the Spirit of God, and I feel that Spirit *after* I have yielded up my heart to God.

I also see this principle manifest in the lives of others who tell how they submitted to God and then received his glorious peace. For example, at our stake conference, Laurie Tueller spoke and described the terrible ordeal of losing her baby Amanda to chronic kidney failure. At Primary Children's Hospital, the doctor gave her the crushing news in a briefing room. After leaving her alone, she fell to her knees and pleaded with God, asking him not to take her baby. She told him she could not handle such a trial. Of her pain she said, "I felt the most heavy darkness in my soul."

Nevertheless, she said, "After several discussions with my husband and many sincere prayers, I finally concluded that if it was

God's will that Amanda should die, then I would be willing to give her up."

Laurie testified of our Father's transcendent love by saying, "When I finally allowed myself to submit to God's will, I felt an overwhelming sense of peace. That heavy darkness was replaced by a calm and reassuring peace that came flooding over me. And I wish I could describe that feeling to you. The fear left me, and I felt the love and concern of my Heavenly Father."

Some months later, Amanda passed away in Primary Children's Intensive Care Unit. But our Heavenly Father healed Laurie's heart, and she said, "I can testify to you, I have never felt the Spirit as strong as I did that night as Amanda passed through the veil. It was a beautiful and sacred experience. And despite all the tears, I felt such a great peace. And it was during this greatest trial that I felt my Savior the closest."

Submission can open our hearts to the Spirit of God and his divine help, while resistance can seal the heavens against us. As King Benjamin said, it is a tendency of the natural man to fight against God. As you might expect, this resistance offends our Father, who said that "rebellion is as the sin of witchcraft, and stubbornness is as iniquity and idolatry" (1 Sam. 15:23). Resistance or stubbornness is manifest in a variety of ways and shows up constantly in our lives. It shows up in our failure to acknowledge God's blessings in our lives. It shows up in our failure to seek or heed his counsel. It shows up in our disobedience to him.

It also shows up in our indifference to him. Sometimes people quit praying because God hasn't answered their prayers in just the way they want. They conclude, with some resentment, that their desires are not important to our Heavenly Father. They say to themselves, "Whatever happens is God's will, so why bother to pray?" Of course to think this really isn't submission at all.

Resentment, murmuring, and withdrawing from God all demonstrate resistance to Heavenly Father's will and a lack of faith in the power of prayer.

Abraham was not afraid to assert his own will in his prayers. Nevertheless, he did so humbly and was ever ready to relinquish his own point of view to match the Lord's. Consider his negotiation with God about the destruction of Sodom and Gomorrah in the eighteenth chapter of Genesis. Notice his words, the last time he asks for fewer righteous persons to be required to save the cities. "And he said, Oh let not the Lord be angry, and I will speak yet but this once: Peradventure ten shall be found there. And [the Lord] said, I will not destroy it for ten's sake" (Gen. 18:32). When we are seeking righteous desires, our will and the Lord's are likely to be the same, but we do need to recognize when the matter is no longer open for discussion.

I would like to suggest that we manifest true submission, or yielding to God, in at least three ways. There may be others, but these three are clearly important to our Heavenly Father. First, we submit to God by recognizing his hand in all things and by thanking and praising him for his blessings. Our Father requires it and we clearly owe it to him. Remember that to submit means to render the things that are required and owed. Thanking and praising God are ways of saying, "Heavenly Father, I am happy with what thou hast done for me. I am happy with thy will." To withhold this thanksgiving is offensive and provokes his anger.

Second, we submit to God by seeking his will. Third, we submit to God by obeying his will. The word *submit* means to be obedient as well as humble.[7] The apostle James said to be "doers of the word, and not hearers only, deceiving your own selves. . . . [B]ut a doer of the work, this man shall be blessed in his deed" (James 1:22, 25). Disobedience can be a manifestation of anything from simple thoughtlessness to disrespect or even rebellion, but none of these sins is likely to incline God to help us. As the Lord revealed:

> *And in nothing doth man offend God, or against none is his wrath kindled, save those who confess not his hand in all things, and obey not his commandments. (D&C 59:21).*

We Submit to Our Heavenly Father by Thanking Him for His Blessings

One of the biggest reasons we don't get more miracles is that we don't recognize or appreciate the ones we already have. We don't give the fitting and required credit to God. Thanksgiving, praise, glory, and credit are things we owe our Heavenly Father, and they are things he requires of us. Thankfulness simply acknowledges our debt to God. A lack of thankfulness tells him either that we think that we owe him nothing at all or that we don't appreciate what he has given us. To credit a blessing to our own hard work is a denial of the truth. It robs us of honest humility and it robs God of the appreciation we owe him. Such a course is not likely to encourage his help.

When we are ungrateful, God sees our rudeness. Remember the time Christ healed the ten lepers? Only one returned to glorify and thank him. Then Jesus asked, "Were there not ten cleansed? but where are the nine?" (Luke 17:12–19). How would Jesus have responded if those nine approached him with another request? How about the one who did thank him? Don't you think God would be open to creating more miracles for him? Jesus bid the man arise and said, "Go thy way: thy faith hath made thee whole" (Luke 17:19).

God allowed Gideon only 300 men to go up against a vast host of Midianites. He said to Gideon, "The people that are with thee are too many for me to give the Midianites into their hands, lest Israel vaunt themselves against me, saying, Mine own hand hath saved me" (Judg. 7:2).

If God cut the number of Israelites from 32,000 to 300, just to ensure that Israel wouldn't claim the credit for themselves, then it must be very tempting to believe happy events are the result of our own work, effort, and strength. But notice also that God says that if the Israelites stole his glory, in effect, they would be vaunting themselves *against him!* Can you imagine the seriousness of being found in opposition to our Heavenly Father, of denying that his help has been important or has been given?

We are clearly submitting to the will of God only when we are genuinely grateful for what he has given us. To complain about God's gifts angers him. It may even provoke him to remove blessings or replace them with punishments.

For example, the Lord miraculously freed the Israelites from slavery to the Egyptians. Then he fed them every day in the wilderness with manna. He gave them water from a rock and extended the life of their shoes and clothes. Yet in spite of all his blessings, the children of Israel complained about their lot again and again. Moses said that "when the people complained, it displeased the Lord; and the Lord heard it; and his anger was kindled; and the fire of the Lord burnt among them, and consumed them that were in the uttermost parts of the camp" (Num. 11:1).

Why should our Father give us more blessings if we can't or won't recognize the ones we already have? In short, an important part of submissive prayer is to recognize and praise God for our blessings. The ability to recognize a miracle is usually necessary to invite more miracles. God gives miracles to those who appreciate the ones they already have.

A child's request is often a pleasure to fill when that child is appreciative, but it's a drag when the child isn't. I remember one occasion when I took my four children to see a movie they especially wanted to see, but when it ended only one of my children remembered to thank me. One not only forgot to thank me but threw a tantrum when he didn't get some candy. At that moment, I was sorry I'd taken him to the movie. I wonder how Heavenly Father feels about handling new requests without receiving any appreciation for requests he has previously filled. A genuinely grateful prayer must be a very refreshing change for him.

As a Navy chaplain at Pearl Harbor, I often led Protestant worship services at the brig, which is a military jail. Mandatory confinement is no great experience, and many prisoners felt that God had abandoned them. Some harbored bitter feelings and forgot their blessings. I would occasionally ask them, "Which of you would sacrifice *both* of your *eyes* to get out of here?" No one ever said yes. They had forgotten the miracle of vision and other blessings as well.

I often told them about a U.S. military ship which pulled into a Japanese port. The ship was surrounded by barges packed with Japanese who were going to clean, scrape, and paint the ship for the privilege of eating the kitchen garbage.[8] I would point out that the brig confinees had hot fresh meals, clean beds, warm clothes, hot daily showers, television, free time for basketball, volleyball, letter writing, visiting with friends, etc. Yes, the quality of their lives had fallen and their freedoms were temporarily restricted, but our Father hadn't abandoned them, and they still had many blessings.

We need to understand how blessed we really are. We are affluent people, and if you don't think so, try answering these questions:

1. Do you have more than one pair of shoes?
2. Do you have more than one choice about what you will eat for each meal?
3. Do you have access to your own means of transportation?
4. Do you have more than one set of underwear?

If you answered "yes" to three or more of these questions, then by the overall standards of the world, you are affluent.

Fewer than 10 percent of all the people who have ever lived have been able to answer "yes" to three or more of these questions at any one time in their lives.[9]

It's wrong to forget our blessings. Nobody likes ingratitude: not you, not me and certainly not the Lord, who has commanded us "to give thanks in all things" (Mosiah 26:39).

Although we so often fail to rejoice in our blessings, the irony is that doing so can be a powerful antidote for unhappiness. One doctor prescribed six weeks of saying thank you for those caught in worry and self-doubt. Within that time most of his patients who applied the prescription lost their worries and doubts.[10] More than once, I have knelt with great burdens and felt God prompt me to thank him for my blessings. As I remembered them I grew so happy I forgot my problems. I would just say, "Thanks, Father. I've got everything I need." I couldn't remember what had depressed me. The Lord said:

> *And he who receiveth all things with thankfulness shall be made glorious; and the things of this earth shall be added unto him, even an hundred fold, yea, more.*
> (D&C 78:19)

We are blessed when we thank, praise, and worship Heavenly Father for his kindness because when he sees that we recognize and appreciate his hand in our lives, then he knows we're ready for more blessings. He knows we won't be spoiled. Alma tells us to "live in thanksgiving daily, for the many mercies and blessings which [God] doth bestow upon you" (Alma 34:38). President J. Reuben Clark said, "Hold fast to the blessings which God has provided for you. Yours is not the task to gain them, they are here; *yours is the part of cherishing them.*"[11]

The "Hallelujah Chorus" from Handel's *Messiah* is one of the most stirring examples of praise ever written. The word *hallelujah* is found in many psalms. Its derivation is Hebrew, and the first portion, *halal,* means "to praise." The final portion, *jah,* stands for the letters *JHVW,* which is the Hebrew symbol for Jehovah. *Hallelujah* means, literally, "to praise Jehovah."[12] The Psalms are full of praise for the Lord, and the words you will find in them are good examples to use in your prayers. Consider the last verse in the very last psalm. "Let every thing that hath breath praise the Lord. Praise ye the Lord" (Ps. 150:6). Indeed, try the interesting experiment of starting with the 150th Psalm and working your way backward through the psalms to see how much they praise the Lord.

To begin with praise and gratitude may be a new way of praying for you. It may require some divine help just to change your order of prayer. Ask Heavenly Father to help you see your blessings and recount them. I often ask him to help me remember each of his blessings, and I name them one by one. As I do that, something inside me changes. My frustrations lift, and I begin to see how much God has cared for me already. I begin to see his interest in my life. I can feel his Spirit working within my soul, and I can, if I listen intently, begin to hear the still, small voice of God which speaks to bless our lives.

We Submit to Our Heavenly Father by Seeking His Will

Elijah discovered our Father's quiet voice when he ran for his life from Queen Jezebel, who vowed to kill him. He journeyed to Horeb, the mount of God, "unto a cave, and lodged there."

Our Father asked, "What doest thou here, Elijah?"

And Elijah responded,

> *I have been very jealous for the Lord God of hosts: for the children of Israel have forsaken thy covenant, thrown down thine altars, and slain thy prophets with the sword; and I, even I only, am left; and they seek my life, to take it away.*

And [God] said, Go forth, and stand upon the mount before the Lord. And behold, the Lord passed by, and a great and strong wind rent the mountains, and brake in pieces the rocks before the Lord; but the Lord was not in the wind: and after the wind an earthquake; but the Lord was not in the earthquake;

And after the earthquake a fire; but the Lord was not in the fire: and after the fire a still small voice. (1 Kgs. 19:9–12)

The writer says that after Elijah *heard* the voice, the Lord sent him on another assignment with assurances that he wasn't alone. Another writer, who described Christ's personal visit to the inhabitants of ancient America, said, "they heard a voice as if it came out of heaven . . . and it was not a harsh voice, neither was it a loud voice; nevertheless, and notwithstanding it being a small voice it did pierce them that did hear to the center . . . yea, it did pierce them to the very soul, and did cause their hearts to burn" (3 Ne. 11:3). To Nephi, Lehi, and their captors in the prison, our Father's voice was "not a voice of thunder, neither was it a voice of a great tumultuous noise, but behold, it was a still voice of perfect mildness, as if it had been a whisper, and it did pierce even to the very soul" (Hel. 5:30).

God usually speaks softly, in a voice like a whisper, and we have to listen to hear him. When we speak in loving tones to close friends, dropping the volume of our voices creates intimate conversation where friends get to know each other better. Heavenly Father likes to speak intimately with those who want to hear what he has to say and with those who believe he is real and capable of speaking. Thus, when he speaks quietly it separates those who really want to hear him from those who are simply seeking a sign.

To recognize the quiet whisperings of the Lord amid the confusion of life, we have to stop and listen. We can train ourselves to hear the quietest sounds of importance if we'll only *listen*. I once read a story of a young man who answered an ad for a telegraph operator's job at a train station. The waiting hall was filled with noisy people waiting for their connection. As he settled down to wait for his interview, he heard a faint sound—the sound of a telegraph clicking out the following message in Morse code: "The first person who hears this message and reports it to the telegraph office gets the job." He reported the message and got the job—because he listened.[13]

Just as you can train yourself to hear and understand the clicks of Morse code in a busy train station, so you can also train yourself to hear the still small voice of God. But you'll need to *stop* and *listen* because the world clatters constantly and interferes with the softer, intuitive side of life. We need to break from the busy clamor of life and create a silent space wherein our Lord can talk to us. Margaret Johnston wrote that "when disaster strikes on British navy vessels, [the boatswain pipes the sound for silence called] 'The Still . . . ' It means, 'Prepare to do the wise thing.'"[14] And so it is in stillness that we learn to hear the personal instruction of God so that we can do the wise thing.

We are so prone to speak that our Father has to coach us to listen. Did you ever notice how he precedes so many of his direct messages with a command to hear?

> *Give ear, O ye heavens, and I will speak; and hear, O earth, the words of my mouth.* (Deut. 32:1)

> *Hear, O heavens, and give ear, O earth; for the Lord hath spoken.* (Isa. 1:2)

> *Incline your ear, and come unto me: hear, and your soul shall live.* (Isa. 55:3)

Why should God speak to me if I won't listen? Suppose in a phone conversation with my parents I asked for help but hung up before they could respond? How could I receive their answer? How could they help me? As a marriage counselor I often saw couples who wouldn't listen to each other. While one spoke, the other prepared a defense. Time and again I would see one spouse speak and then the other would respond as if he or she hadn't heard a word the other had said. It's not possible to build an intimate relationship without listening. Intimate relationships are built on mutual listening which manifests mutual regard and respect.

The Bible prophets built their relationship with our Heavenly Father by listening to him. As a young boy, Samuel's mother gave him to the Lord and took him to Eli for training in the Lord's ways. During his training, Samuel was taught to listen by Eli, the High Priest of the Tabernacle. During the night Samuel heard his name called, and he ran to Eli who told him, "if he call thee, . . . thou shalt say, Speak, Lord; *for thy servant heareth*" (1 Sam. 3:9; emphasis mine). Samuel followed these instructions, and hearing the Lord's voice, he "let none of [God's] words fall to the ground" (1 Sam. 3:19).

When we listen, God urges us to obey his commandments. This is the main task of the still, small voice—to strengthen our consciences. Everyone can hear this still, small voice, and when we listen for it, we should expect to hear about our sins and to receive guidance toward "right" living. Stephen R. Covey was addressing a group of college students on the importance of chastity before marriage. As they discussed it, the audience resisted his arguments. Two of the students were notably effective in their opposition. Brother Covey finally asked the students to be still for a moment and *listen.* He said if they didn't inwardly sense the truth of his words, he would stop wasting their time. When they were still, he asked them whether chastity, as he'd explained it, was a true principle. After a full minute of silence, he turned to one of the young antagonists and asked him what he had felt and heard. The young man replied, "What I heard is not what I've been saying."[15]

We Submit to Our Heavenly Father by Doing His Will

When we begin listening to Heavenly Father, we will often hear him prompt us to repent. When we refuse to obey God's commandments, we are sending a nonverbal message that we don't respect his counsel or guidance. We are rejecting him as our God. If we don't heed his calls to repent, the Lord may conclude that we really don't care to hear what he has to say. He may stop speaking to us until we do repent. God has said:

> *No matter how much you pray, I will not listen, for your hands are covered with blood.*
>
> *Wash yourselves clean. Stop all this evil that I see you doing. Yes, stop doing evil and learn to do right . . .*
>
> *If you will only obey me, you will eat the good things the land produces.*
>
> *But if you defy me, you are doomed to die.* (Isa. 1:14–20; Today's English Version)

So often then, the first miracle we need to seek is the miracle of repentance and obedience. The biggest mistake we could make would be to delay our prayers until we feel totally worthy. Perhaps the most important function of prayer is to help us in the repentance process. Even a desire to repent, or a decision to repent, begins to pull the powers of heaven closer to us and makes it possible for us to receive the spiritual power we need to cleanse our lives and increase the probability that our other prayers will be heard. When we are on the path of righteousness, desiring and seeking his cleansing power in our lives, we can look confidently to God for the miracle of forgiveness and then for other miracles. Sin and an unrepentant attitude destroys our spiritual inclinations and interferes with our ability to communicate spiritually with God and our ability to receive miracles from him. This may seem obvious in the case of big sins but not so obvious for little sins. Nevertheless, any lack of submission in our lives can hinder or even block our communion with God. The spiritual process of repentance, which manifests our submission, brings us closer to God.

> *The Lord is far from the wicked: but he heareth the prayer of the righteous. (Prov. 15:29)*

> *And the Redeemer shall come to Zion, and unto them that turn from transgression. (Isa. 59:20)*

John the beloved apostle said, "Whatsoever we ask, we receive of him because we keep his commandments, and do those things that are pleasing in his sight" (1 John 3:22). James the brother of Christ said, "The effectual fervent prayer of a righteous man availeth much" (James 5:16). Doesn't it seem logical that Father will test our obedience before he blesses us? If we hear and obey our consciences, we get the miracles. He "[hears] the prayer of the righteous" (Pro. 15:29) and counsels, "seek ye first the kingdom of God, and his righteousness; and all these things shall be added unto you" (Matt. 6:33). We are blessed when we obey.

Heavenly Father cares about our moral behavior and works to develop it because life is about choosing good over evil. This is taught throughout scripture and is felt whenever we listen to our consciences. Have you ever argued with someone about something you thought was right? Can you remember how strong your feelings were? Sometimes the argument about right and wrong can be a burning issue. C.S. Lewis said that the fact that we argue about what's right is compelling evidence of our deep moral nature.[16] Even criminals care enough about "being right" to deny or rationalize wrongdoing.

John Steinbeck was one of our greatest American writers. In one of his finest novels, *East of Eden,* he used the beginning of chapter thirty-four to ask the question, "What is the world's story about?" He answers by saying that there is only one story in life and that it encompasses and transcends every aspect of our lives.

In every dimension of experience, we are entangled in a web which continually confronts us with moral choices. "Virtue and vice," he said, "were warp and woof of our first consciousness, and they will be the fabric of our last. . . . There is no other story. A man, after he has brushed off the dust and chips of his life, will have left only the hard clean questions: Was it good or was it evil? Have I done well—or ill?"[17]

Warp and *woof* are terms used in weaving. The warp is "the threads running lengthwise in the loom,"[18] while the woof is "the horizontal thread crossing the warp in a woven fabric."[19] These threads are carried through the warp with a shuttle and are woven together with the warp into fabric. Any cutting out or unweaving weakens, damages, or destroys the fabric. Hence the warp is sometimes referred to as "the very fiber or essential part of something; [the] foundation [or] base."[20] The notions of virtue and vice are woven into the very fabric of our souls from the beginning to the end of our existence. Our souls are lifted and strengthened by our virtuous choices, and conversely, our souls are pained and diminished by choosing vice.

Our Heavenly Father built virtue and vice detectors into the fibers of our souls. The biologist Lewis Thomas described one such *right and wrong* detector that is built into our minds and sends alarms throughout our bodies. He said we "cannot tell a lie, even a small one, without setting off a kind of smoke alarm somewhere deep in a dark lobule of the brain. . . . The outcome, recorded by the lie-detector gadgetry, is a highly reproducible cascade of changes in the electrical conductivity of the skin, the heart rate, and the manner of breathing, similar to the responses to the various kinds of stress." According to Lewis Thomas, even if we lie for pleasure, blaring signals are sent screaming throughout our bodies, warning us that something is wrong. Physiologically, lying is not natural;[21] it is stressful.

How could it be otherwise? Our Heavenly Father is a God of Truth, and as his children, we inherit a need to live in truth. We hurt ourselves when we lie, and we hurt ourselves any time we sin because "every sin is a lie."[22] Sins deliver something very different from what they promise. They are illusions. If we were to look closely, we would discover that every one of Satan's tempting reasons to disobey God's commandments is a lie which will degrade our lives if we believe it.

Our Heavenly Father sent us here to learn his way of life, and he won't begin to move powerfully in our behalf, beyond helping us to repent, until we are cleansed of our sins. When Jesus visited the Nephites in America, observers there recorded that "there was not any man who could do a miracle in the name of Jesus save he were cleansed every whit from his iniquity" (3 Ne. 8:1). Aleksandr Solzhenitsyn observed the hope that many cancer patients had for a remission from their disease. Podduyev, a patient who had no hope, reasoned, "I suppose for that you need to have . . . a clear conscience."[23] Podduyev is right. We need to have a clear conscience to effectively exercise our hope and faith in God. Some people confuse this clear conscience—achieved by daily repenting and weekly renewing of our baptismal covenants—with the virtually impossible goal of "being perfect" in mortality. We don't need to be perfect in order to exercise powerful faith in our prayers, but we do need to be made clean through Christ.

We have no need to be afraid of the principle of repentance. The word *repent* merely means "to change." It is taken from the Greek word *metanoia.* The first part, *meta,* means "change," and the second part, *noia,* means "spirit." The word literally means to change your spirit or to change your mind. If you think about it, this is only logical. God constantly works to help us become more like him. It must be obvious that to become more like him we would need to change and adopt his ways. That, basically, is repentance.

Perhaps it will help to think of our sins as mistakes. John Wycliffe was the first person to translate the Bible into English. From the Latin Bible, the Vulgate, he translated the word *peccatum* as *sin,* but *peccatum* meant "error" or "fault." The Hebrew Bible used the word *ahvoair,* which meant "missing the mark."[24] Doesn't it lift your sense of hope to honestly think of sins as mistakes to be corrected? Our Heavenly Father doesn't expect us to face our sins alone. He wants to help us overcome them. He can hold us accountable for our sins because he will "prepare a way for [us] that [we] may accomplish the thing which he commandeth [us]" (1 Ne. 3:7). Our Heavenly Father will show us our weaknesses and help us overcome them.

Suggestions for Repentance

1. *Pray for divine guidance.* Jesus said, "And if men come unto me *I will show unto them their weakness.* I give unto men weakness that they may be humble; and my grace is sufficient for all men that humble themselves before me; for if they humble themselves before me, and have faith in me, then will I make weak things become strong unto them" (Ether 12:27; emphasis mine).

The apostle Paul said, "But let a man examine himself" (1 Cor. 11:28). Later he wrote more specifically, saying, "Examine yourselves, whether ye be in the faith" (2 Cor. 13:5). This honest, conscience-directed self-examination will reveal "your iniquities [which] have separated between you and your God, and your sins [which] have hid his face from you, that he will not hear" (Isa. 59:2).

As Alma told his son Corianton, "let your sins trouble you, with that trouble which will bring you down unto repentance" (Alma 42:29). Our Heavenly Father will help us see our most serious weaknesses and sins; things that when fixed will prepare us to meet him. This revelatory self-review is the beginning of repentance and greater obedience.

2. *Proceed one step at a time.* Since we've too much repentance to accomplish all at once, our Father in Heaven will break it down into smaller parts and show us where to start. He doesn't expect us to change everything in one day and will work with us as our capacity develops. He treats us like a good parent would treat any child, expecting only what is appropriate for our age and maturity, expecting less of children who are younger in the faith.

Think of a baseball coach who accurately assesses the maturity and skill level of his players and expects them to play up to that level. Your Heavenly Father is like a good coach who knows what your moral capabilities are and expects only the appropriate amount of effort and change from you. He'll teach you a little at a time as you are able to bear it: "For precept must be upon precept, precept upon precept; line upon line, line upon line; here a little, and there a little" (see Isa. 28: 9–13; 2 Ne. 28:30; D&C 98:12; 128:21).

3. *Examine your thoughts and feelings, as well as your actions.* Alma said that "our words will condemn us, yea, all our works will condemn us; . . . *and our thoughts* will also condemn us" (Alma 12:14; emphasis mine). The Lord sent the great flood because "the wickedness of man was great in the earth, and that every imagination of the thoughts of his heart was only evil continually" (Gen. 6:5). Evil begins in the heart and the mind.

Christ said "that whosoever looketh on a woman to lust after her hath committed adultery with her already in his heart" (Matt. 5:28). In the Beatitudes he said: "Blessed are the pure in heart: for they shall see God" (Matt. 5:8). Paul said that charity, which is the pure love of Christ (Moro. 7:47), "thinketh no evil" (1 Cor. 13:5). This principle is a key to communion with God, who tells us, "Let virtue garnish thy thoughts unceasingly; then shall thy confidence wax strong in the presence of God" (D&C 121:45). Heavenly Father will guide us in reviewing our thoughts and our beliefs as well as our words and our actions.

4. Seek charity, the pure love of Christ. "Thou shalt love the Lord thy God with all thy heart, and with all thy soul, and with all thy mind. This is the first and great commandment" (Matt. 22:37–38). It is critical to bring God into the center of our lives. Ask yourself how much thought, love, or worship you have given our Heavenly Father lately. How often do you think about him? What do you think about him? How do you feel about him? Do you really listen to him and talk to him?

Pray for the gift of charity. Moroni said, "Pray unto the Father with all the energy of heart, that ye may be filled with this love, which he hath bestowed upon all who are true followers of his Son, Jesus Christ" (Moro. 7:48).

5. Use the Golden Rule. "Therefore all things whatsoever ye would that men should do to you, do ye even so to them: for this is the law and the prophets" (Matt. 7:12). The Golden Rule is so important that it is a foundation belief of every major world religion. "Hurt not others with that which pains yourself" (Buddhism). "Do not unto others what you would not they should do unto you" (Confucianism). "What is hurtful to yourself do not to your fellow man. That is the whole of the Torah and the remainder is but commentary. Go and learn it" (Hebraism). "This is the sum of duty: do naught to others which if done to thee, would cause thee pain" (Hinduism). "No one of you is a believer until he loves for his brother what he loves for himself" (Islam).[25]

Jesus said that the second most important commandment, after love of God, is "Thou shalt love thy neighbor as thyself. On these two commandments hang all the law and the prophets" (Matt. 22:37–40). Elder James E. Talmage, a great Latter-day Saint apostle, emphasized that "honesty of purpose, integrity of soul, individual purity, . . . willingness to do good to all men even enemies, pure benevolence—these are some of the fruits by which the religion of Christ may be known, far exceeding in importance and value the promulgation of dogmas and the enunciation of theories."[26]

In the Book of Mormon, Ammon said, "Now my brethren, we see that God is mindful of every people" (Alma 26:37). Be honest with others because you would want others to be honest with you. Repent of any dishonesties you discover in yourself. Be faithful to your spouse because you would like him or her to be faithful to you. Serve others as you would like to be served yourself. Love others as you would like to be loved by them. Forgive others as you would like to be forgiven by them and as you would like to be forgiven by God. Our Lord has said, "For if ye forgive men their trespasses, your heavenly Father will also forgive you: But if ye forgive not men their trespasses, neither will your Father forgive your trespasses" (Matt. 6:14–15). In the Beatitudes he said: "Blessed are the merciful; for they shall obtain mercy" (Matt. 5:7). How we treat God's children is tantamount to how we treat our Savior, who said, "Inasmuch as ye have done it unto one of the least of these my brethren, ye have done it unto me" (Matt. 25:40).

6. *Use the Ten Commandments and the Sermon on the Mount.* Most of the instructions within them were given to explain the Golden Rule. They are mainly clarifications on how to help God's children or avoid harming them. His children are our brothers and sisters. Our Heavenly Father provided these commandments because he knows better than anyone else what will help his children and what will hurt them. We cannot violate these rules and draw close to our Father in Heaven. We must keep these commandments to please him.

7. *Ask Heavenly Father to help you keep his commandments.* Our Heavenly Father is always ready to help us repent if we ask for his help. Successful members of Alcoholics Anonymous say they "humbly asked Him to remove [their] shortcomings."[27]

Elder James E. Faust told how God helped tannery workers

keep the Sabbath day holy. He said that J. Lowell Fox, the supervisor of the Wells Stake Welfare Tannery, reported a miracle that occurred on every Sabbath. Every day but Sunday, animal hides had to be taken from the vats so that the lime solution could be replaced. When this didn't happen the hides spoiled. This had to be done every day, except Sunday.[28] Think about it. What stopped the microbes on Sunday? This is miraculous help.

All of our Father's commandments are important enough for him to change chemical and biological processes to help us keep them, so if we asked him, wouldn't he also change our minds and hearts?

I read an article about a man who thought there was no pleasure in some commandments, such as attending church, but he wanted to change that attitude. Morning and night he began to ask the Lord to bless him to feel about church services the way the Lord felt about them and to be able to participate in them the way he would. Over a period of time, his feelings did change. He said "Sunday became a day filled with light." No longer was attending church a matter of suppressing unrighteous desires but "an expression of righteous, loving desires."[29]

This man used prayer to obtain divine changes in his heart. I experimented with this kind of prayer and found it works. I discovered that if I humbly sought his help, God could change my feelings and give me joy in living a particular commandment.

It may take days or weeks or months of pleading with the Lord, but principle by principle, we can learn to love the things God loves, through prayer. I testify that God can and will change our hearts if we pray with faith and continue to press forward.

Our Savior fasted and prayed forty days and nights seeking God's strength. We know he prayed for his apostles that their faith would not fail. Christ demonstrated the importance of such prayer by saying, "And lead us not into temptation, but deliver us from evil" (Matt. 6:13). If he needed our Father's help, don't we need divine help that much more?

Even though Christ was tempted, even with all manner of temptations (see Alma 7:11), he "gave no heed unto them" (D&C 20:22). We are not supposed to tinker with temptation. God can hold us accountable for any dalliance with it because he has the power to help us overcome it. Elder Maxwell said of Jesus, "Unlike some of us, He did not fantasize, reconsider, or replay temptations. How is it that you and I do not see that while initially we are stronger and the temptations weaker, dalliance turns things upside down?"[30] We should follow Christ's example and always seek our Heavenly Father's divine help in prayer to resist temptation.

Even charity, the pure love of Christ, is a gift of God. This love comes only from our Heavenly Father. Moroni said we are nothing without charity, but "whoso is found possessed of it at the last day, it shall be well with him. Wherefore, my beloved brethren, pray unto the Father with all the energy of heart, that ye may be filled with this love, which he hath bestowed upon all who are true followers of his Son, Jesus Christ" (Moro. 7:47–48).

Forgiving another of a deep wrong or loving a bitter enemy might be impossible without prayer, yet Christ said, "Love your enemies, bless them that curse you, do good to them that hate you, and pray for them which despitefully use you, and persecute you. That ye may be the children of your Father which is in heaven. . . . For if ye love them which love you, what reward have ye? do not even the publicans the same? And if ye salute your brethren only, what do ye more than others? Do not even the publicans so?" (Matt. 5:44–47). If you need a miracle in your heart to forgive someone, ask for it. Learn to love your enemies by praying for them. Ask God to help you to understand them and fill your heart with love toward them. Ask him to soften their hearts toward you, and as you do this your heart will be purified and you will find yourself drawn to your Father in Heaven.

8. *Don't give up.* The Lord may require our obedience for some time to show that our repentance is sincere. Time may also be required for deep cleansing to occur. One time the Lord told the Saints that they "were slow to hearken unto the voice of the Lord their God; therefore, the Lord their God [was] slow to hearken unto their prayers, to answer them in the day of their trouble. In the day of their peace they esteemed lightly [his] counsel; but, in the day of their trouble, of necessity they [felt] after [him]" (D&C 101:7–8).

9. *Practice repentance every day.* Repentance works wonders when instituted as a daily practice. It's like washing or bathing each day. It keeps the soul in tip-top readiness to meet with God. Our souls are like our bodies—they feel better when they're clean. Dirt can make us feel scummy and cause infections. That's why most of us bathe regularly. We need it. Oil collects on our skin and in our hair and then dust and dirt attach to it. This mixes with perspiration, and then bacteria begin to grow. So we wash because it feels good to be clean.

I'll never forget a little story from the book *Shogun,* by James Clavell. Blackthorne is a Dutch navigator aboard a seventeenth-century English vessel which is wrecked in a storm off Japan. In Europe at that time, bathing was not a common practice, and though the sailors are not aware of it, their foulness makes them repugnant to the Japanese. Blackthorne is separated from his companions and is taught Japanese customs, one of which is the practice of frequent bathing. After a long time, Blackthorne visits his old shipmates and is appalled at the personal filth and squalor he finds them living in. He is disgusted, until he remembers that he once lived that same way. Seeing clearly the value of cleanliness, he knows he can never go back to his old ways.

I can relate to his decision. I have gone to the field with the Army and lived without showering for nearly two weeks. When we were returning home the only thing I could think about was a hot shower. The feeling of cleanliness is wonderful when you get used to it. Our sins are like dirt and filth which collect invisibly inside us and make us feel unclean. This is a great burden to carry, once we begin to notice it.

Some psychologists would teach us to ignore these feelings, but if we did that, we would be like Blackthorne's shipmates—we would simply be ignorant of our filth. It certainly is possible to live with our filth, but imagine the consequences of being filthy before God and not knowing it. I believe we are foolish to assume we are clean before God. To be absolutely certain, our souls need to be washed clean in the atonement of Christ every day. We need to recognize the dirt of our sins and the guilt accumulating in our souls. To be cleansed, we need to repent and come unto Christ for the grace of his cleansing atonement. This he symbolized so eloquently by washing his disciples' feet. These were the best men of his time, and they still needed Christ's cleansing to be free from the blood of their sins. Our sins are real and they cling to our souls in the same way that dirt, sweat, and oil cling to our skin and hair. Sin needs to be washed away before we can feel clean and pure before the Lord.

10. *Confess major sins to appropriate religious authority.* The apostle James said, "Confess your faults one to another, and pray one for another, that ye may be healed" (James 5:16). It is not good to be so concerned about our image that we cannot humbly acknowledge to others the weaknesses or failings which are common to all of us. The problem with the Pharisees of Christ's time was their constant concern about putting forth the "appearance of righteousness." They loved to look good. Furthermore, some sins are of such importance, or our difficulties overcoming them are so

great, that we really need the help of someone who has been properly called of God to be a judge in Israel. This is your bishop or stake president.

To begin the process of repentance, listen to your conscience. Start your repentance and look forward to God's warm response. Remember that when the prodigal son returned home, the father *ran* out to meet him and fell on his neck and kissed him and killed the fatted calf in celebration (Luke 15:20–24). To desire divine guidance requires the humble faith that God knows what is best, and that requires finding and purging the evil from our hearts. If time is short, our Heavenly Father might delay this requirement, but he wants us to repent, and he will run to greet us warmly on our journey home.

We need to submit to our Heavenly Father first. It's a big mistake to skip this step. So thank our Father sincerely for each of your blessings. Pause and praise him before you weep and wail. Listen for his will, which is your divine homework. Inventory and confess each of your sins. Sincerely seek his help through prayer to aid you in the repentance process; then strive each day to obey Father's commandments, and you will begin to receive his most precious blessings.

Notes

1. Lee Dalton, "View from Above," *New Era,* October 1981, 8–10.
2. Frederick C. Mish, ed., *Webster's Ninth New Collegiate Dictionary* (Springfield, MA: Merriam-Webster Inc., 1984), 1175.
3. Ibid., 1368.
4. Ibid.
5. Neil Flinders, Class notes.
6. *Webster's Ninth,* 1368.
7. David B. Guralnik, ed., *Webster's New World Dictionary of the English Language,* 2nd college ed. (Cleveland: William Collins & World Publishing Co., Inc., 1974), 1418–19.
8. Charles R. Swindoll, *Growing Strong in the Seasons of Life* (Portland, OR: Multnomah Press, 1990), 289.

9. Stephen Glenn and Jane Nelson, *Raising Self-Reliant Children in a Self-Indulgent World* (Rocklin, CA: Prima Publishing and Communications, 1989), 44–45; emphasis mine.
10. Fred Bauer, "Thanks for Everything," *Reader's Digest*, November 1994, 172.
11. J. Reuben Clark, *Church News,* June 14, 1969, 2; emphasis mine.
12. Old Testament Student Manual Genesis–2 Samuel (Salt Lake City: The Church of Jesus Christ of Latter-day Saints, 1980), 309. See also, Old Testament Gospel Doctrine Teacher's Manual (Salt Lake City: The Church of Jesus Christ of Latter-day Saints, 1989).
13. William W. McDermet III, *The Upper Room,* vol. 50, no. 3, Jul-Aug 1984, 50.
14. Margaret Blair Johnston, "Sanctuary—The Secret of a Peaceful Heart," *Reader's Digest*, January 1961, 31.
15. Stephen R. Covey, *The Divine Center* (Salt Lake City: Bookcraft, 1982), 181–82.
16. C. S. Lewis, *Mere Christianity* (New York: MacMillan Publishing Co., Inc., 1960), 17ff.
17. John Steinbeck, *East of Eden* (Chicago: Sears Readers Club, 1952), 413.
18. *Webster's New World Dictionary*, 2nd college ed., 1602.
19. Ibid., 1637.
20. Ibid., 1607.
21. Lewis Thomas, "Late Night Thoughts on Listening to Mahler's Ninth Symphony," 128. In Henry B. Eyring, BYU Devotional Address, 18 November 1986, "Going Home," 12–13.
22. Neil J. Flinders, *Teach the Children: an Agency Approach to Education* (Provo, Utah: Book of Mormon Research Foundation, 1990), 49.
23. In Bernie Siegel, *Love, Medicine, and Miracles* (New York: Harper & Row Publishers, 1986), 7.
24. Cliff C. Jones, *Winning through Integrity* (New York: Ballantine Books, 1985), 5.
25. Selwyn Gurney Champion, *The Eleven Religions and Their Proverbial Lore* (New York: E.P. Dutton & Co., Inc., 1945), xviii; emphasis mine.
26. James E. Talmage, *Articles of Faith* 12th ed. (Salt Lake City: The Church of Jesus Christ of Latter-day Saints, 1968), 429.
27. *Alcoholics Anonymous* (New York: Alcoholics Anonymous World Services, Inc., 1976), 59.
28. James E. Faust, "The Lord's Day," *Ensign,* November 1991, 35.
29. Dennis R. Peterson, "To Love the Things God Loves," *Ensign,* March 1981, 6–7.
30. Neal A. Maxwell, *Ensign,* May 1989, 64.

5

Request Specific Blessings in Faith

The Second Scripture Continued

> *Give us this day our daily bread.*
> *And forgive us our debts, as we forgive our debtors.*
> *And lead us not into temptation, but deliver us from evil:*
> *For thine is the kingdom, and the power, and the glory, for ever.*
> *Amen. (Matt. 6:11–13)*

Step Three

Here in the last part of his prayer, we see Jesus ask for blessings after he knew his Father's will. He seeks his own desires and needs last and then asks only for essentials. He requests food, forgiveness, and goodness. He seeks "first the kingdom of God, and his righteousness" (Matt. 6:33) and shows us what to seek. James said, "Ye ask, and receive not, because ye ask amiss" (James 4:3). Another reason we "receive not" is insufficient faith.

The Third Scripture

> *If any of you lack wisdom, let him ask of God, that giveth to all men liberally, and upbraideth not; and it shall be given him.*
>
> *But let him ask in faith, nothing wavering. For he that wavereth is like a wave of the sea driven with the wind and tossed.*
>
> *For let not that man think that he shall receive any thing of the Lord.* (James 1:5-7)

God gives to all of his children generously. Ask him in faith without *wavering, and you will* receive good things. If you waver, you will get nothing from the Lord. Faith is "an unquestioning belief in God."[1] It is complete trust in or loyalty to him. It is our conviction that he is real, which we manifest with all of our heart, might, mind, and strength. It is our full confidence in his goodness and our absolute reliance on his help and instructions. Faith is the unique combination of belief, hope [desire], and trust.

Faith is belief. Our beliefs are affairs of the intellect. They are thoughts or ideas that we accept as true. Our beliefs precede our actions but don't guarantee that we will act. For example, if I *believe* in theory that I can build my own house, but I'm not sure of my skills, commitment, or resources, I may lack the confidence necessary to risk my time, effort, and money. To only *think* I can build a house isn't the same as to *know* I can build a house. My intellectual *belief* is, therefore, inconsequential because I won't build a house just because I *think* I can do it. It is true that I can't or won't build a house unless I believe it's possible for me to do so. Nevertheless, believing in the possibility is not enough and it's not a complete faith. Only real faith, complete faith, will motivate us to action, and neither I nor most folks will try to build a house on mere theory. The apostle James noticed this "inconsequence of mere belief"[2] and commented, "Thou believest that there is one

God; thou doest well: the devils also believe, and tremble" (James 2:19). The devils believe there is one God, but that knowledge does not motivate righteous actions. Intellectual belief alone isn't enough to get me to build a house.

Faith is hope. A complete faith includes a deep and driving desire. This is hope, which is the next thing I need. To hope is "to want very much."³ It's a desire for something, accompanied by some confidence in the belief that it can be realized. Paul said, "Faith is the substance of things *hoped for*" (Heb. 11:1; emphasis mine). Without hope or desire, I won't lift a finger to build my own home. If I don't *want* to build my own house, or if I don't *want* it enough to expend the effort or money, I'll never do it. Hope is more than a wish. True hope motivates you to pay whatever righteous price is necessary. Where there is no hope, there is no faith. Moroni said: "If a man have faith he must needs have hope" (Moro. 7:42). By itself, hope isn't faith, but when it is combined with belief and trust, the three become faith. As part of our religious faith, we hope for life hereafter in the celestial kingdom through faith in Jesus Christ. But the scriptures also give clear examples of hoping for many other righteous rewards.

Faith is trust. While our beliefs are affairs of the intellect, our trust is an affair of the heart. Trust is so much more than mere intellectual assent. It is also more than the mere absence of worry, which might only be the absence of desire. Paul said that "faith is the substance of things hoped for" (Heb. 11:1). When translated from the Greek manuscripts, the word for *substance* means "assurance" and *assurance* is "sureness; confidence; certainty."⁴ A synonym for *assurance* is *trust*.⁵ It is firm confidence or *assurance* or *trust* which enables a person to act and take risks. For example, a tour guide at a mint took his group to the cauldrons of molten metal. He told them he could pour red-hot metal onto their hands and they wouldn't feel anything *if* their hands were wet. Then he asked a couple if they would like to try it. The husband said, "No, thank you, I'll take your word for it." But his wife responded . . . "Sure, I'll give it a try!" She then dipped her hand into a bucket of water and held it out to test the claim. "The hot liquid rolled off harmlessly just as the guide said it would."6 The husband said he believed, but who do you think trusted the guide and *really* had faith in his words?

Phillips Brooks said, "The first faith is the easy, traditional belief of childhood, taken from other people, believed because it belonged to the time and land. The second faith is the personal conviction of the soul. . . . It is the heart knowing, because God has spoken to it, the things of God."7 The first faith is easy belief, but the second faith is the potent combination of belief, hope, and trust. When we willingly surrender to God, trusting completely in his power and goodwill toward us, we are experiencing the second faith. Then our soul discovers the "reality that enables a man to stand anything that can happen to him"8 and moves us to bet our lives on Heavenly Father.

Trust is the necessary foundation for an intimate and lasting relationship with God. In truth, no intimate relationship is possible without it. Have you ever seen happily married couples who *didn't* trust each other? You can't have a close relationship with someone you don't trust. Trusting couples share sensitive feelings with each other. Their trust helps them listen and respond with respect. This creates a loving, lasting bond. The more they trust, the more they become one. Our relationship with Heavenly Father needs to be like that of trusting couples because we love and unite with him as we trust him. In a relationship with God, the need for trust may be even greater than it is for couples. That's why God will test your faith before he grants your request.

> *I will try the faith of my people. (3 Ne. 26:11)*

> *Ye receive no witness until after the trial of your faith.* *(Ether 12:6 [1-40])*

Try their faith . . . then shall the greater things be made manifest unto them. (3 Ne. 26:9)

There are several ways you can measure your faith. One way is to look at your obedience to God's commandments. When we don't trust Heavenly Father, we are judging some of his commandments by saying, "No, that's not important." But this response shows we trust ourselves more than we trust Heavenly Father. We think we know better than he does, and this is a most dangerous form of skepticism. Obedience requires a great deal of trust. Do I trust the Lord enough to pay an honest tithe and keep the Sabbath day holy? Do I trust him enough to search his scriptures every day? Do we trust him enough to love and serve our fellowman as he commands? The more we trust and obey our Father, the greater is our bond.

There are other ways to check our faith. God can look at our willingness to be humble and to repent. He can see how long our faith lasts. He can observe whether we pursue our righteous desires through afflictions and obstacles. He can assess how or if we endure our trials. But we need to check our own faith. Are we wavering in the feelings of our *hearts?* Do we feel confident? Are we hesitating to use all of our *might* or resources? How are we using our assets to pursue our desires? Are we wavering in the thoughts of our *minds?* Do we visualize the miracle we desire and hold its vision in our thoughts? Are we hesitating to use our *strength* or personal energy? What are we doing to obtain our desires? When we are in tune with the will of God and exercise our faith with all of our *heart, might, mind,* and *strength*—then in God's time, we'll get our miracle.

We need faith enough to recognize God's answers and respect his wisdom and perfect timing. Sometimes we think things have to be done at a certain time or in a certain way, yet there can be many ways to get the job done. The Lord's thoughts are not our thoughts. He likes to answer our prayers in creative ways and often answers through small and simple means with miracles that are easy to overlook.

Alma referred to the Liahona, a brass compass that worked by faith. A spindle would point in the direction Lehi's party was to go, and writing would appear on the ball as needed. It was a miracle repeated day after day through which the Lord guided Lehi and his family through the wilderness. However, "because those miracles [the Liahona] worked by small means. . . . [the Nephites] were slothful, and forgot to exercise their faith and diligence and then those marvelous [but small] works ceased, and they did not progress in their journey" (Alma 37:41).

Sometimes we just don't recognize the miracles we receive or have the patience to wait for our answers. It takes faith to see small miracles, just as it takes faith to wait for them. I once asked for a certain job because I needed the money. I didn't get the job, but I got the money I needed later in a different way. The Lord said, "It is my purpose to provide for my saints. . . . But it must needs be done in mine own way" (D&C 104:15–16) and "in mine own due time" (D&C 35:25).

Faith Creates the Miracle

You may ask why our Father would require us to have faith *before* granting a request? Wouldn't a little demonstration give us faith? Couldn't he prove himself with a miracle for a sign? History illustrates the ineffectiveness of miracles shown to the faithless. Heavenly Father gave the pharaoh in Egypt ten miraculous demonstrations of his power, and the pharaoh didn't respect any of them. Even after losing his eldest son, the pharaoh changed his mind and sent armies to the Red Sea in pursuit of the Israelites. *Even the children of Israel,* who also saw the miracles, had so little faith that they constantly murmured and rebelled in the wilderness.

At one point Moses lamented that they wanted to stone him (Ex. 17:4). Their rebellion was so consistent, even after seeing numerous miracles, that the Lord had to raise up a new generation with greater faith to take into the promised land. It is vital to note that this generation with greater *faith* hadn't seen the miracles in Egypt.

Because miracles don't create faith, unless he has a specific purpose God first requires our faith in him and then he rewards it. This is common sense. Because God wants to develop our faith, it follows that he must reward us when we show faith. To create a miracle in the absence of faith is to reward the absence of faith. Should he reward our doubt? If he answers our prayers when our faith wavers, then he would be rewarding wavering faith. Such a reward would allow us to assume that partial confidence was sufficient. He would be limiting our ability to exercise real faith.

I learned the basics of this principle in my schoolwork. One of my college projects required me to train a mouse to feed itself by pressing a lever. Every day I took my mouse from its cage to the Skinner Box. The Skinner Box is a special cage with a metal wall on one side and a horizontal bar protruding through an opening in the wall. When the bar was pressed down, it released a pellet of mouse food into the feeding dish below.

The first time my mouse touched the bar, I manually released a pellet into his feeding tray, hoping he would see the connection between the depressed bar and the released pellet. Although my mouse had touched the bar, he still *had not pressed* it down, and this was a critical point in the experiment. If I gave him a pellet too many times before he actually pressed the bar, he wouldn't learn how to do it himself. So the second time he touched the bar, I didn't release a pellet. The mouse kept on experimenting and finally put his weight on the bar, pressed it down, and clicked out a pellet. From that point on, he ate whenever he wanted.

Some of the students' mice wouldn't press the bar because their student trainers gave them pellets each time they *approached* it. These trainers were well-intentioned, but their mice learned something very different about the bar and pellets than mine did. Their mice learned to get a pellet by *approaching* the bar. My mouse learned to get a pellet by *pressing* the bar. My mouse learned to feed himself, but their mice never did. If Heavenly Father gave us miracles before we obtained the required faith, then we might think that we only need to *approach* the bar with belief or hope. Yet we really need to *press* the bar with faith to get the miraculous pellet.[9]

From this experiment I learned to give rewards *after* performances are finished. Suppose I gave my son a candy bar for washing the dishes before he did the job? Without any other intervention on my part, would the dishes get done? Your guess is as good as mine. Most employers never pay a man before he has worked. Most paychecks follow the employee's service anywhere from one to thirty days after the work is done.

Our Heavenly Father doesn't make miracles to create our faith. He makes miracles to reward our faith. Moroni asked, "Has the day of miracles ceased?" And then he answered his own question, "Behold I say unto you, Nay; . . . if these things have ceased wo be unto the children of men, for it is because of unbelief" (Moro. 7:35–37). Elsewhere in the scriptures we read:

> *As thou hast believed, so be it done unto thee. (Matt. 8:13)*

> *Thy faith hath made thee whole. (Matt. 9:22)*

> *If ye have faith as a grain of mustard seed, ye shall say unto this mountain, Remove hence to yonder place; and it shall remove; and nothing shall be impossible unto you. (Matt. 17:20)*

If faith is what we lack, then faith is the first miracle we must seek, and God has given us ways to obtain it. Believing in God isn't hard. Gallup polls suggest that more than 90% of Americans believe in God.[10] If you can believe in a God who created us, it's just a small step further in logic to conclude that he can accomplish whatever he wants. If it is his will, he can certainly make your miracle. If we believe he *can* make our miracle, why then do we waver or doubt? Knowing why we doubt will suggest ways to reduce or eliminate wavering doubt and produce rocklike faith.

We waver about his will. We're not sure he *will* make our miracle. We believe or even know he can, but we're not sure he will! Our belief in his power is okay, but our ignorance of *his* point of view or *will* is creating a doubt or wavering that looks something like this:

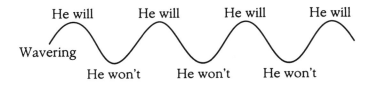

How, then, do we find out if he *will?* The solution here is to learn what our Heavenly Father really thinks about our request. We have to go back to step two in our prayer and *ask him.* We have to ask him, and then we have to *listen* to his spiritual promptings. We have to listen better so we can hear and understand him. We have to *know* his will. Then we have to obey him. If you are wavering in your faith, go back to the Lord and listen. Inquire of him. Consult with him and seek his will. Visit with him as often as necessary to *find out* what he is *thinking!*

Take your notebook and pencil with you, and go back to the second step of listening in your prayer. You'll need the notebook to write down the impressions that will come as you listen. Your Father won't want to repeat himself, so be like Samuel, and don't let any of his words fall to the ground. Record your Father's promptings. If you fail to record his promptings and then forget them, our Heavenly Father can conclude that you're not interested in what he has to say.

Once you *know* your desire is good because you've *heard* God confirm it, you will be able to pursue it with the great confidence necessary to produce your miracle. This brings you back to the second step again—listening. Be prepared to write because you're probably going to receive instructions. Elder Boyd K. Packer had a friend who suffered catastrophic financial reverses in his business, "and there just didn't seem to be any way out." He began to rise at 3 A.M. "with a paper and a pen" to "ponder and pray and write down every idea that came to him."

> It wasn't long before he had several possible directions in which he could go, and it wasn't much longer than that until he had chosen the best of them. But he had earned an extra bonus. His notes showed, after he went over them, that he had discovered many hidden resources he had never noticed before. He came away more independent and successful than he would ever have been if he hadn't suffered those reverses.
>
> There's a lesson in this experience. A year or two later he was called to preside over a mission overseas. His business was so independent and well set up that when he came back he didn't return to it. He now has someone else managing it, and he is able to give virtually all his time to the blessing of others.[11]

Heavenly Father can't speak to us in this way if we're not prepared to hear him. Elder Richard G. Scott believes that "we often leave the most precious personal direction of the Spirit unheard because we do not *record* and respond to the first promptings that come."[12] We wouldn't have the scriptures if someone hadn't recorded the prophets' revelations and miracles. A new bishop learned to pray by listening with a pencil and a notebook. He found it was easier to commune with the Lord if he talked less and listened more. Each morning, he pondered the scriptures until he felt ready to pray. He soon learned that "a pen and a pad of paper were necessary to write down the ideas as they came. The promptings proved valuable as [he reorganized] ward auxiliaries and issued call after call to people who knew of their new callings before they were made."[13]

We waver, wondering if our desire is good. We need divine help to evaluate our requests, so check out each request. Is it righteous? Is it selfish? Is it necessary or expedient? Is it moral? Is it in harmony with gospel principles? Does it infringe on the free agency of others? How does it compare with the Savior's requests in the Lord's Prayer? Here again the solution is to go back and check it out with God. Keep listening until you know his will. Study his guiding principles as they are recorded in the scriptures. We have to search the scriptures and listen to our conscience to know what is right.

> *[God] doth grant unto you whatsoever ye ask that is right.* (*Mosiah 4:21*)

> *Trifle not with these things; do not ask for that which you ought not.* (*D&C 8:10*)

> *And Christ hath said: If ye will have faith in me ye shall have power to do whatsoever thing is expedient.* (*Moro. 7:33*)

> *And if ye ask anything that is not expedient for you, it shall turn unto your condemnation.* (*D&C 88:65*)

We waver, wondering about our worthiness. This is why we need to humble ourselves before our Maker in confession and make serious commitments to listen, repent, and obey. Righteousness pleases the Lord, and we might have to be obedient long enough to show the Lord we're serious. Elder Boyd K. Packer said in response to this worry, "It may be that you are not doing anything wrong. It may be that you have not done the right things long enough. Remember, you cannot force spiritual things."[14] Don't get impatient with the Lord. He does things in his own due time, and he also tests our faith. Remember, "ye receive no witness until *after* the trial of your faith" (Ether 12:6; emphasis mine). But remember also that "whosoever shall put their trust in God shall be supported in their trials" (Alma 36:3). You "shall be delivered out of your trials . . . and ye shall be lifted up at the last day" (Alma 38:5).

We waver in our desire. We're not willing to pay the price. Desire is so much more than just a wish, and sometimes we find that we've never really wanted anything beyond the basics of an easy, pleasant life. We may not want something enough to sacrifice interfering desires that compete for our hearts and minds. We can waver in our desire by wanting first one thing and then another or by wanting too many things all at once. We can also be unsure about what we really want, although we might be unsure about a desire because we lack faith. If we aren't sure we can get it, we might tell ourselves we don't want it.

A clear, strong desire is like a laser light, which is monochromatic, something very different from the polychromatic light given off in the lightbulbs of your home. *Poly* means many and *chromatic* refers to wavelength or frequency. A standard polychromatic lightbulb gives off light in all directions and wavelength colors of the light spectrum. This mixture lights our homes and offices, but it is too weak to be projected to the moon, cut through steel, or repair torn tissues in the eye. It is too weak because its energy is dissipated in all directions and with all wavelengths.

We create laser light by filtering light and focusing it, not by mixing and dissipating it. We capture and use just one wavelength or frequency of light. The laser filters out every lightwave that isn't traveling in the desired direction and at the desired frequency, capturing, holding, and amplifying the desired wavelength until scientists are ready to use it. In a similar way, our thoughts need to be focused on a single desire. The thoughts of our *minds,* the feelings of our *hearts,* the use of our *might* and *strength* need to be focused on a single, clear desire. Once your desire becomes as clear and focused as laser light, you'll be ready to begin to get your miracle. You must know *what* you want before Heavenly Father can give it. That's why he asks, "Behold, what desirest thou?" (1 Ne. 11:2, 10).

A small boy was travelling through the Mojave Desert with his family when their car began overheating. Eighteen miles later, after the car died, this boy said, "Don't worry, Dad. I'm gonna talk with God and ask him to send a bus to get us." He knelt near a highway marker and prayed "with his hand cupped to his ear." He rose after a long time and insisted to his family that a bus was coming up the hill. It appeared almost immediately. The driver said he wasn't supposed to stop because it was against company policy to stop in the desert and he was hours behind schedule. Nevertheless, he said he had felt a prompting. This boy made a laserlike request in simple faith and got a laserlike response to a real need.[15]

Here's another example of the importance of the *specific* request. An elderly investigator stunned her LDS missionaries by refusing to see them anymore. She had studied everything they had given her and attended church meetings faithfully. But she explained that she had lost her glasses and wouldn't be able to read the Book of Mormon without them. Since it was reading that made the Church so meaningful to her, she saw no point in continuing. More importantly, she would lose her job because she could not work without her glasses, and she would never be able to afford another pair in her lifetime. One of the elders promised she would find her glasses if she prayed.

They returned a few days later to find her more discouraged because she had prayed so fervently and received no answer. They asked her *how* she had prayed and found she had sincerely recited all the prayers she had memorized as a child. The missionaries then taught her to pray and ask *specifically* to find her glasses.

They returned a few days later and she asked to be baptized. She told them that when she rose from her prayer, a small strange dog carried her glasses into her home and began playing with them.[16]

The laserlike request is just a small part of the process, but it is important. Ask yourself what you want. What is your hope? Being precise in your request is the only way to recognize when your prayer is answered. What do you want or need to happen? When do you need it to happen? How would you like it to happen? Who do you want it to happen to, etc.? As Alma said, "[God] granteth unto men according to their *desire"* (Alma 29:4; emphasis mine). God himself said to Enos, "I will grant unto thee according to thy *desires,* because of thy faith" (Enos 1:12; emphasis mine). God will even strengthen your righteous desires. Ask him. Listen more and God will make your righteous desires become more like laser light.

We waver because of others' doubts. People affect our thoughts and feelings. Those around us influence us because we're all connected in a vital and spiritual way. The connection is unseen, but real.

The Macaca fuscata is a Japanese monkey that has been observed in its natural setting for over thirty years. In 1952, scientists were giving sweet potatoes to the monkeys on the island of Koshima. One of the monkeys named Imo began to wash her potatoes in a stream, and other young monkeys learned this new practice over a period of years. The adult monkeys, however, refused to adopt the new habit. Then something strange happened in the autumn of 1958. Within a single day, nearly every monkey in the tribe began to wash his or her potatoes. It surprised the scientists to see that colonies of monkeys hundreds of miles away on the mainland and other islands began to wash their potatoes. This occurred despite the fact that there was *no physical contact* between the colonies. This example suggests that a "new awareness may be communicated from mind to mind."[17] Dr. Wayne Dyer said he has heard "scientists in virtually all fields of study talk about the invisible forces that connect all members of a species."[18]

Dr. Srully Blotnik studied worker attitudes for over twenty years and saw the influence of co-workers on each other. He said, "Those around us affect us. And they do so far more than most of us would care to admit."[19] This influence can be either positive or negative. Mormon led the Nephites into battle and prayed for them, yet he did so "without faith, because of the hardness of [the Nephites'] hearts" (Morm. 3:12). Jesus visited his native home and "did not many mighty works there because of their unbelief" (Matt. 13:58).

This social connection is one of the reasons we pray and exercise our faith in behalf of others. If we share our faith, those who are open to it can receive it. If we open ourselves to those with faith, we will receive faith. If we open ourselves to those who doubt, we will receive doubt.

Check out your friends closely, and you'll probably want to spend most of your time with those who are believers. Unite your faith with the faith of others to make it stronger. Don't hang around with skeptics. Surround yourself with people of faith who can lift and inspire you. Read the work of writers who inspire you and avoid those who discourage you. Pay attention to what strengthens or weakens your faith and increase whatever strengthens it and decrease whatever weakens it. Do what you have to do to get more faith.

The Fourth Scripture

Jesus had called his twelve apostles and sent them out two by two to preach the gospel, heal the sick, and cast out evil spirits.

They had apparently had some success because one man brought them his son who was possessed by an evil spirit. When the apostles weren't able to cast the evil spirit out, the man took his son to the Savior and said:

Master, I have brought unto thee my son, which hath a dumb spirit;

And wheresoever he taketh him, he teareth him: and he foameth, and gnasheth with his teeth, and pineth away: and I spake to thy disciples that they should cast him out; and they could not.

He answereth him, and saith, O faithless generation, how long shall I be with you? how long shall I suffer you? bring him unto me.

And they brought him unto him: and when he saw him, straightway the spirit tare him; and he fell on the ground, and wallowed foaming.

And he asked his father, How long is it ago since this came unto him? And he said, Of a child.

And ofttimes it hath cast him into the fire, and into the waters, to destroy him: but if thou canst do any thing, have compassion on us, and help us.

Jesus said unto him, If thou canst believe, all things are possible to him that believeth.

And straightway the father of the child cried out, and said with tears, Lord, I believe; help thou mine unbelief.

When Jesus saw that the people came running together, he rebuked the foul spirit, saying unto him, Thou dumb and deaf spirit, I charge thee, come out of him, and enter no more into him.

And the spirit cried, and rent him sore, and came out of him: and he was as one dead; insomuch that many said, He is dead.

But Jesus took him by the hand, and lifted him up; and he arose.

And when he was come into the house, his disciples asked him privately, Why could not we cast him out?

And he said unto them, This kind can come forth by nothing, but by prayer and fasting. (Mark 9:17–29)

Fasting and Prayer

In verse 23, Christ reiterates that "all things are possible to him that believeth" (Mark 9:23). In verse 24, the father pleads "help thou mine unbelief." He asks Christ to strengthen his faith and the Lord does! The father asks for faith and gets it.

Yet there is one more thing to learn about miracles from this story. The Savior's apostles asked why they couldn't cast out the evil spirit, and Jesus responded, "*This kind* can come forth *by nothing,* but by prayer *and fasting*" (Mark 9:29; emphasis mine). In other words, some kinds of problems are so tough they require prayer *and fasting* to obtain enough faith for the miracle.

President Joseph F. Smith said that the law of the fast "as understood by the authorities of the church, is that food and drink are not to be partaken of for twenty-four hours, . . . and that [we] are to refrain from all bodily gratification and indulgences."[20] This is the same as skipping two full meals. For example, suppose we begin by eating breakfast, then skip lunch and supper and eat breakfast the next day. We have skipped two complete meals and refrained from eating or drinking anything for twenty-four hours.

The spirit of your fast is more important than the letter of the law. When you don't eat or drink anything and prayerfully skip a meal, you are still fasting, though a complete fast would last for twenty-four hours. Sometimes weakness or poor health makes a complete fast infeasible.[21] I also believe that if you forget and accidentally interrupt your fast by eating, you can regroup and continue your fast. Simply express your sorrow to your Heavenly Father and ask him to allow you to continue your fast.

The object of the fast is to refrain from worldly appetites and to devote yourself to God in prayer in order to be better able to hear his words and exercise your faith. A fast should increase our humility before our Heavenly Father, and once this is accomplished, you can focus on communicating your righteous desires to the Lord. In the attitude of fasting we should be more able to check our own desires and be certain they are righteous and in tune with the Lord's will. Unrighteous requests are mistakes that keep us from experiencing miracles, and wavering faith occurs when we don't know the Lord's will. We can humbly learn his will and submit to it with more unwavering faith by combining fasting with our prayers.

Notes

1. David B. Guralnik, ed., *Webster's New World Dictionary of the American Language,* 2nd college ed. (Cleveland: William Collins & World Publishing Co., Inc., 1974), 503.
2. In Obert C. Tanner, *Christ's Ideals for Living* (Salt Lake City: Obert C. and Grace A. Tanner Foundation, 1981), 279.
3. *Webster's New World Dictionary,* 676.
4. Ibid., 84.
5. J. I. Rodale, *The Synonym Finder* (Emmaus, PA: Rodale Press, 1978), 1262.
6. Richard W. DeHaan, *Our Daily Bread,* Dec-Feb 1983-84, December 1.
7. In Tanner, 35.
8. Ibid., 34.
9. This little experience may give the impression that *whenever* we exercise any faith, we receive the reward. Actually, it isn't quite that simple, and this will be made clear in later chapters. God evaluates our needs and the righteousness of our requests, and he may even *increase* the amount of faith he requires from time to time.
10. Tom Minnery, "Want to Live Long? Go to Church," *Focus on the Family Citizen,* May 1989, 3.
11. Boyd K. Packer, *Teach Ye Diligently* (Salt Lake City: Deseret Book, 1975), 204–5.
12. Elder Richard G. Scott, "Spiritual Communication," in *Principles of the Gospel in Practice* (Salt Lake City: Randall Book, 1985), 8; emphasis mine.

13. Richard D. Anthony, "I Was a Bishop before I Really Learned to Pray," *Ensign,* January 1976, 52–53.
14. Elder Boyd K. Packer, Conference Report, October 1979, 29–30.
15. Kathleen Conger Ellis, "Raymond and the Bus," *Ensign,* April 1981, 52–53.
16. Stephen L. Law, "Lost Glasses," *Ensign,* April 1981, 54–55.
17. Ken Keyes, Jr., *The Hundredth Monkey* (Coos Bay, OR: Vision Books, 1981), 11–17.
18. Dr. Wayne R. Dyer, *You'll See It When You Believe It: The Way to Your Personal Transformation* (New York: William Morrow, 1989), 95.
19. Srully Blotnik, *Getting Rich Your Own Way* (New York: Doubleday, 1980), 231.
20. Joseph F. Smith, *Gospel Doctrine* 5th ed. (Salt Lake City: Deseret Book, 1939), 243.
21. For a deeper understanding of the fast, see "Fasting" in Bruce R. McConkie, *Mormon Doctrine* (Salt Lake City: Bookcraft, 1966), 275–77.

6

Remembering Our Father's Son

Step Four

> *O then, my beloved brethren, come unto the Lord, the Holy One. Remember that his paths are righteous. Behold, the way for man is narrow, but it lieth in a straight course before him, and the keeper of the gate is the Holy One of Israel; and he employeth no servant there; and there is none other way save it be by the gate; for he cannot be deceived, for the Lord God is his name. (2 Ne. 9:41)*

A story is told of three men journeying to heaven. When the gates were within view, they paused in thoughtful contemplation. The boldest approached the gatekeeper.

"What do you think of Jesus Christ?" the gatekeeper asked.

The man had no ready answer for this question and was forced to honestly admit, "I don't know. I was so busy at work and other activities that I never thought much about him." The gatekeeper directed him to a waiting place outside the gate.

Having overheard the question and feeling prepared to answer, the second man approached the gate and answered confidently. "I loved the Lord and did many things in his name. I preached the gospel, baptized souls into his kingdom, and healed the sick, all in his name." However, after listening, the gatekeeper directed him to wait outside the gate along with the first man.

The third man, still determined to venture forth, humbly approached the gate. As with the others, the gatekeeper looked at him and asked, "What do you think of Christ?"

In response, he said nothing, but fell at the gatekeeper's feet and worshipped.

He alone *knew* the Savior. And those who know the Savior also know the Father. As Jesus said:

> *I am the way, the truth, and the life: no man cometh unto the Father, but by me.*
>
> *If ye had known me, ye should have known my Father also: and from henceforth ye know him, and have seen him.*
>
> *Philip saith unto him, Lord, shew us the Father, and it sufficeth us.*
>
> *Jesus saith unto him, Have I been so long time with you, and yet hast thou not known me, Philip? he that hath seen me hath seen the Father. (John 14:6–9)*

Furthermore, to know the Father and the Son is to have eternal life. Christ said: "And this is life eternal, that they might know thee the only true God, and Jesus Christ, whom thou hast sent" (John 17:3). Yet how well do we really know the Savior? How much do we think about him or study his teachings? King Benjamin asked: "For how knoweth a man the master whom he has not served, and who is a stranger unto him, and is far from the thoughts and intents of his heart?" (Mosiah 5:13).

What would we know of our own trades if we studied them for as few hours as we may have studied the words and character and actions of Christ? How much achievement would there be in science today if researchers had studied and thought as little about their subjects as some of us have studied and thought about our Master?

Stephen R. Covey, in his book *The Divine Center,* asks us who or what is at the center of our thoughts, our feelings, our study, and our lives. This is an important question to consider. What is the center of our lives? Is it Christ or is it our work? Is it pleasure or possessions? Are we centered on some combination of things? Are we centered on our church? If so, is it more important to be centered on church activities than it is to be centered on Christ? Are we centered on our families? And if so, don't we risk our families when we fail to center them on Christ? A family may enjoy great relationships without Christ, but they cannot be sealed together in his temple. Isn't the Church here to help us bring our families to the Lord?

James Francis said that Christ is "the centerpiece of the human race."[1] Then shouldn't we also make him the centerpiece of our personal lives? Christ is certainly the centerpiece of all the scriptures, especially the Book of Mormon. Another experience I had as a chaplain drove this lesson home for me. When I arrived at the headquarters of the 3rd Marine Infantry Battalion, I introduced myself and got acquainted with each officer. During our visits, nearly every officer asked me, "Have you met Reverend Jones yet?"

When I said no, they responded, "Don't worry, you will."

A Marine battalion consists of about 750 men divided into five companies. Reverend Jones was assigned to Lima Company, and I inquired among the enlisted Marines to learn more about him. They told me he was on leave (as was most of the battalion) following a six-month deployment they had just completed. He was a Marine corporal who had been a former drug addict. He had made a dramatic shift in his life when he was converted to Christ and released from his addiction to drugs. Since that time he had become a persuasive lay minister. The Marines called him "Reverend" because he spent most of his spare time preaching and testifying of Christ. To those who weren't interested in his message (which was most of the battalion), he was like a mosquito they brushed aside. Nevertheless, he had some followers who banded with him to try and reach the others.

When I finally met him at the recreation offices two weeks later, he was ironing a uniform for an inspection the next morning. He seemed pleased to see me and asked a few questions about the scriptures. Then he showed me a lesson plan from a Bible class and asked me what I thought about it. I made a comment he seemed to like, and then he asked which church I attended. When I told him "Mormon," he remained cordial and seemed to know nothing about our faith. Soon, he left for a revival meeting at some place he called the Eagle's Nest, a place for Evangelical worship and fellowship.

He attended all my worship services in the field for about six months until the day he saw a virulent anti-Mormon movie at the Eagle's Nest. From then on he refused to attend my services and sought to persuade others that Mormonism was of the devil. About a year passed, and our battalion boarded three troop-carrying assault ships to spend six months in the Pacific. Corporal Jones and I were assigned to different ships. I rode the largest troop transport, which was a giant ship nearly 900 feet long and looked much like a small aircraft carrier. Instead of planes, it carried helicopters, trucks, and about 2,600 men.

As our six-month tour neared its end, I was reassigned to a smaller ship for our two week return trip to Hawaii. This happened to be the ship where "Reverend" Jones was assigned. During the trip I asked him to attend my services, but he refused. He had given me and others aboard ship some ugly anti-Mormon literature. Furthermore, he had persuaded the ship's Protestant lay leader and nearly all the active Protestants on board ship that Mormons weren't Christians, and so they also refused to attend.

I began to pray because I didn't know what else to do. I knew I would only be aboard ship with him for one more week, and I wanted him to see the truth. Being frustrated and humbled, I began to pray more fervently. "Heavenly Father, he has been misguided and spread a lot of lies, but we were once friends, and I want him to know the truth about thee and thy church. What can I do?"

I continued to pray about this for several days until a calm spirit settled in my heart. Then came a distinct impression to show him the testimony of Christ in the Book of Mormon. I was to let the book speak for itself about the Savior. This answer seemed too simple, but the impression persisted, and I began to study the book's testimony of Christ more closely. During this study I discovered a seemingly endless number of passages which testified of Christ, directly and powerfully. And so I prayerfully prepared to show this testimony to Reverend Jones and others.

The ship's Protestant lay leader was the first person to examine the Book of Mormon for himself. First I bore a strong testimony of our Lord and attributed my testimony of Christ to the Book of Mormon. Then I showed him the book's introduction and many of the Book of Mormon verses which testified so powerfully of Christ. After seeing the truth, he decided to support me and convinced a few of the other Protestants to attend my church services.

Reverend Jones wasn't as open-minded as the Protestant lay leader had been, so I prepared for our meeting with fasting and prayer. I asked the Lord to bless us that he would listen to me and let me show him the Book of Mormon's powerful testimony of Christ. Since Corporal Jones led his own church services in a dirty and uncomfortable part of the ship, I decided to let him use my office for his services.

When he called at my stateroom to return the key to my office,

I invited him in and said sincerely, "I believe that the movie you saw and the literature you've been distributing doesn't square with the truth. I know Christ is my Savior and have been taught that from my youth. May I ask why you think our faith is of the devil?"

He responded with a difficult question, but I chose to avoid an argument and said, "I don't know the answer to your question, but I do know that Jesus Christ is my Lord and Savior. I have learned that from the Book of Mormon, which was written to bring us to Christ. I've been a member of LDS congregations in many areas of the world. I've served as a missionary for two years and graduated from our formal religious training programs. I believe I know what is commonly taught in our church. This Book of Mormon [which I cradled in my hands] is our standard for doctrine, and I'd like you to see for yourself what it says about Jesus Christ. May I show it to you and let you judge for yourself?"

After a pause he consented, and then I showed him the translated preface in which I had highlighted: "to the convincing of the Jew and Gentile that JESUS is the CHRIST, the ETERNAL GOD." Then I showed him the passage where Paul said that "no man can say that Jesus is the Lord, but by the Holy Ghost" (1 Cor. 12:3). To strengthen his understanding of the Bible I had him read John's words: "Hereby know ye the Spirit of God: Every spirit that confesseth that Jesus Christ is come in the flesh is of God" (1 John 4:2). And finally a Book of Mormon scripture: "For every thing which inviteth to do good, and to persuade to believe in Christ, is sent forth by the power and gift of Christ; wherefore ye may know with a perfect knowledge it is of God" (Moro. 7:16).

Then we sat side by side while I turned to what might have been an entry in Nephi's journal and read:

> *And we talk of Christ, we rejoice in Christ, we preach of*
> *Christ, we prophesy of Christ, and we write according to our*

prophecies, that our children may know to what source they may look for a remission of their sins. (2 Ne. 25:26)

We continued to read Book of Mormon scriptures which testified of our Savior. Nephi wrote often of Christ in his records, and he wrote to testify of Christ's grace to his people.

And I, Nephi, have written these things unto my people, that I might persuade them that they would remember the Lord their Redeemer. (1 Ne. 19:18)

Behold, my soul delighteth in proving unto my people the truth of the coming of Christ. . . .
And my soul delighteth in proving unto my people that save Christ should come all men must perish. (2 Ne. 11:4, 6)

I explained that before his death, Nephi passed his writings to his brother Jacob and commanded him to record sacred preaching and revelation and hand them down from generation to generation "for Christ's sake, and for the sake of [the] people" (Jacob 1:3–4).

And he [Nephi] gave me, Jacob, a commandment that I should write upon these plates a few of the things which I considered to be most precious. (Jacob 1:2)

Wherefore we labored diligently among our people, that we might persuade them to come unto Christ, . . .
that all men would believe in Christ, and view his death, and suffer his cross and bear the shame of the world. (Jacob 1:7–8)

I told him that this tradition of maintaining the record continued to the end of the Book of Mormon. After Christ's crucifixion and resurrection, he visited ancient America. He descended from heaven and spoke unto the people, saying:

Behold, I am Jesus Christ, whom the prophets testified shall come into the world.
And behold, I am the light and the life of the world; and I have drunk out of that bitter cup which the Father hath given

*me, and have glorified the Father in taking upon me the sins of
the world, in the which I have suffered the will of the Father in
all things from the beginning.*

*Arise and come forth unto me, that ye may thrust your hands
into my side, and also that ye may feel the prints of the nails in
my hands and in my feet, that ye may know that I am the God
of Israel, and the God of the whole earth, and have been slain
for the sins of the world. (3 Ne. 11:1–14)*

We read scripture after scripture. We read until Reverend Jones
seemed spiritually sated. He could hold no more. So I took him
to the last page and told him about Moroni, who was the last
prophet to write in the Book of Mormon. I noted that Moroni
watched the destruction of his civilized nation because the people
rejected Christ and his teachings. Then I showed him Moroni's
plea, the closing witness of the Book of Mormon.

*Yea, come unto Christ, and be perfected in him, and deny
yourselves of all ungodliness . . . that by his grace ye may be
perfect in Christ. . . .*

*And again, if ye by the grace of God are perfect in Christ,
and deny not his power, then are ye sanctified in Christ by the
grace of God, through the shedding of the blood of Christ, which
is in the covenant of the Father unto the remission of your sins,
that ye become holy, without spot. (Moro. 10:32–33)*

I said, "The Book of Mormon is our scripture. It begins with
Christ. It continues with Christ. It ends with Christ. It refers to
Christ 'more frequently per verse'[2] than even the New Testament.
Its record of Christ's visit to America establishes his concern for
all people and even its final words call us to him." I paused and
watched while Corporal Jones pondered, staring intently at the
scriptures before him.

After a long silence he said, "I guess I'll have to read the Book
of Mormon. Do you have another copy?"

That was my last day aboard his ship. As I left the following morning though, he and one of his friends met me on the dock to express their friendship and wish me well. Then they departed for Waikiki. I never saw either of them again, but the marvelous testimonies of Christ found in the Book of Mormon enabled us to part as friends, and they enabled Reverend Jones to see the Book of Mormon in an entirely new light. I also know that the Book of Mormon brought me closer to Christ than I had ever thought possible. The Lord had answered my prayers with divine precision and opened my eyes to see the importance of Christ as I had never seen him before.

Elder Bruce R. McConkie declared that our life's goal is "to have God into our souls, to have the love of Christ in our hearts. It is to have the mind of Christ—to think what he thinks, say what he says, believe what he believes, and . . . do what he does."[3]

How important is it to appreciate the suffering of our Father's Son? Our sins are offensive to God, but we are "reconciled unto him through the atonement of Christ" (Jacob 4:11), which was Christ's divine suffering for our sins to satisfy the law of justice. Alma said "there is a law given, and a punishment affixed, and a repentance granted; which repentance, mercy claimeth; otherwise, justice claimeth the creature and executeth the law, and the law inflicteth the punishment; if not so, the works of justice would be destroyed, and God would cease to be God" (Alma 42:22).

Therefore, our Father sent his Son, Jesus Christ, to make that payment for us if we would repent and keep his commandments. Christ then made an atonement for our sins. According to Webster, an atonement is "satisfaction given for wrongdoing, injury, etc."[4] Because Christ made amends for us, his "mercy claimeth the penitent" (Alma 42:23). Christ has become our mediator and advocate with the Father. Paul said we are "justified by his blood" (Rom. 5:9), and King Benjamin said the "blood of Christ atoneth for [our] sins"

(Mosiah 3:16). He has offered to redeem us from our punishments if we repent and seek his forgiveness. Otherwise we are spiritually obligated to pay for our own sins. If I understand the scriptures correctly, that price is enormous.

When Martin Harris lost the 116 pages of manuscript for the Book of Mormon, the Lord spoke to him directly through Joseph Smith and said:

> *Therefore I command you to repent—repent, lest I smite you by the rod of my mouth, and by my wrath, and by my anger, and your sufferings be sore—how sore you know not, how exquisite you know not, yea, how hard to bear you know not.*
>
> *For behold, I, God, have suffered these things for all, that they might not suffer if they would repent;*
>
> *But if they would not repent they must suffer even as I;*
>
> *Which suffering caused myself, even God, the greatest of all, to tremble because of pain, and to bleed at every pore, and to suffer both body and spirit—and would that I might not drink the bitter cup, and shrink—*
>
> *Nevertheless, glory be to the Father, and I partook and finished my preparations unto the children of men.*
>
> *Wherefore, I command you again to repent, lest I humble you with my almighty power; and that you confess your sins, lest you suffer these punishments of which I have spoken, of which in the smallest, yea, even in the least degree you have tasted at the time I withdrew my spirit. (D&C 19:15–20)*

The Lord is our Savior because he suffered the punishment for our sins. He literally paid for our sins to satisfy the law of justice. Our Heavenly Father loves him dearly, not only because he was our Father's Only Begotten Son but because Christ willingly gave his life and suffered so much that it caused him, "even God, the greatest of all, to tremble because of pain."

Elder Neal A. Maxwell said that the Savior suffered for more than the punishment for our sins. "All our infirmities and sicknesses were somehow, too, a part of the awful arithmetic of the Atonement. . . . His suffering—as it were, *enormity* multiplied by *infinity*—evoked His later soul-cry on the cross, and it was a cry of forsakenness."5

Stephen Robinson says this in another way:

> God uses no magic wand to simply wave bad things into nonexistence. The sins that he remits, he remits by making them his own and suffering them. The pain and heartaches that he relieves, he relieves by suffering them himself. These things can be shared and absorbed, but they cannot be simply wished or waved away. They must be suffered. Thus we owe him not only for our spiritual cleansing from sin, but for our physical, mental, and emotional healings as well, for he has borne these infirmities for us as well.6

With Christ as our mediator, our Heavenly Father will do things for us even though we may be unworthy because he deeply loves his Son. As parents, we do the same thing. My children have made requests which I've refused until my wife, whom I dearly love, has interceded. Because I love her so much, I have often granted the requests of our children for no other reason than her influence. When our children please their mother, they please me as well. And I believe the principle is the same with our Father, who commands us to make our requests in the name of his Beloved Son, Jesus Christ.

Elder James E. Talmage pointed out that "Christ is a sacred title, and not an ordinary appellation or common name; it is of Greek derivation, and in meaning is identical with its Hebrew equivalent *Messiah* or *Messias*, signifying the *Anointed One*."7 Christ has been anointed by our Father. How should this knowledge affect our prayers? How should it affect our thoughts and feelings about Christ? How often should we think lovingly and reverently of Christ? More is implied here than just voicing Christ's name.

Do we feel deep appreciation for him each time we use his name in prayer? Moroni said that the judgment bar of God will go well for anyone who has the pure love of Christ (Moro. 7:47). Surely we not only need the ability to love as the Savior does, but we also need to love the Savior with a pure love. And so we must "pray unto the Father with all the energy of heart, that [we] may be filled with this love, which he hath bestowed upon all who are true followers of his Son, Jesus Christ" (Moro. 7:48).

Using his name with great love will help us keep our lives divinely centered. In the Lord's prayer, Christ prayed directly to his Father, so he doesn't include his own name. He needs no intermediary with the Father. He is our intercessor with the Father. In other scriptures, our Lord has clearly directed us to use his name in prayer.

The prophet Nephi said that "ye must not perform any thing unto the Lord save in the first place ye shall pray unto the Father *in the name of Christ,* that he will consecrate thy performance unto thee, that thy performance may be for the welfare of thy soul" (2 Ne. 32:9; emphasis mine). And marvelous is the promise he makes to those who prayerfully use his name in doing his will: "And whatsoever ye shall ask in my name, that will I do" (John 14:13–14; 15:16).

Notes

1. In Obert C. Tanner, *Christ's Ideals for Living* (Salt Lake City: The Obert C. and Grace A. Tanner Foundation, 1981), 6.
2. Ezra Taft Benson, "Come unto Christ," *Ensign,* November 1987, 83.
3. Bruce R. McConkie, "How to Worship," *BYU Speeches of the Year,* 20 July 1971, 7.
4. David B. Guralnik, ed., *Webster's New World Dictionary of the American Language,* 2nd college ed. (Cleveland: William Collins & World Publishing Co., Inc., 1974), 88.
5. Neal A. Maxwell, "Willing to Submit," *Ensign,* May 1985, 73.
6. Stephen E. Robinson, *Believing Christ* (Salt Lake City: Deseret Book, 1992), 123.
7. James E. Talmage, *Jesus the Christ* (Salt Lake City: Deseret Book, 1970), 35–36.

The Road to Faith in God

Two roads diverged in a wood, and I—
I took the one less traveled by,
and that has made all the difference.

—Robert Frost

ROADS CONNECT US TO CITIES AND DESTINATIONS, BUT NOT every destination is a physical location. When we choose a journey on the path of faith, we are led to spiritual destinations where we can connect with God. Although we may not arrive at perfect communion with him during our lifetime, we can expect to get much closer to him than we are now.

On the path of faith we can learn to seek righteous miracles with confidence. We can also learn to acquire strength or wisdom beyond our normal abilities. Through our faith, God can greatly increase spiritual influences to soften the hearts of our husbands or wives, children or parents, friends or enemies whenever they choose to be receptive. We can learn to develop confidence in

Heavenly Father's decisions. We can learn that he created life for our happiness. The path of faith leads to your Father and mine, the Creator of our lives. It leads to his power, the power that created the universe.

The *Lectures on Faith* teach that "faith . . . is the first great governing principle which has power, dominion, and authority over all things; by it they exist, by it they are upheld, by it they are changed, or by it they remain, agreeable to the will of God. Without it there is no power, and without power there could be no creation nor existence!"[1]

If deep, life-changing belief "has power, dominion, and authority over all things," why do we resist choosing this road? And why do we want the miracles without the journey?

Part of the reason is that this road isn't wide and smooth. It isn't paved. We can't ride in our cars. It really is a narrow way, a path which climbs steeply upward. We must climb, and as we do, the path leads to challenges which we can only overcome with our Father's help. There will be swinging footbridges hanging across deep chasms which will force us to make "leaps of faith" in order to move closer to God. You must cross the chasms of time and place and person. For example, it's good to believe God made miracles for the prophets in Palestine more than two thousand years ago. It's also good to believe he made a miracle for your friend in Salt Lake City last year. But it's best (and hardest) to believe he'll make a miracle for you, here and now. You must move from believing in the miracles given to *them*, *there* and *then,* to believing in the miracles God can make for *you, here* and *now.* Some people call this jump the "leap of faith."

Our journey on this road is also going to be resisted by a being who knows the destination and blessings of this trail and doesn't want us to know our Heavenly Father. He is Satan, and the scriptures are loaded with testimony of his existence and intent.

And the Lord said, Simon, Simon, behold, Satan hath desired to have you, that he may sift you as wheat:

But I have prayed for thee, that thy faith fail not. (Luke 22:31–32)

And there was war in heaven: Michael and his angels fought against the dragon; and the dragon fought and his angels,

And prevailed not; neither was their place found any more in heaven.

And the great dragon was cast out, that old serpent, called the Devil, and Satan, which deceiveth the whole world: he was cast out into the earth, and his angels were cast out with him. (Rev. 12:7–9)

There are nearly one hundred scriptures referring to Satan. Christ clearly testified of real confrontations with Satan, and his disciples recorded them. I've always believed Satan was real because of those accounts, but I never really thought about his possible influence over me in the here and now until I was stationed in Germany. While there I became close friends with another army sergeant named Charlie Black. He and his wife arrived in Augsburg at about the same time as my wife and I, and we began spending a lot of time together. Charlie and I were assigned to the same unit for more than a year. When I was called to serve as bishop of the Augsburg Serviceman's Ward, he was called to serve as my first counselor. He had traveled a rather rocky road prior to making his gospel commitment, but at that time he was well along the road of faith.

In May of 1977, shortly before we began serving together in the bishopric, he had gone to the Bavarian forests on a military exercise. That first night, the sky was clear, the air was warm, and he was very tired, so he didn't bother to set up his little pup tent. He chose instead to roll out his sleeping bag in a clearing on a slight slope with his head under a majestic old tree.

As dawn approached he was enjoying a pleasant dream when something warned him of danger. He awoke with a start and sat up to see five men squatting around his sleeping bag. Another man standing behind the five seemed to be in charge. They were so close he could have reached out from his bag and touched them. Instantly he was wide awake and he knew he was surrounded by an enemy. There was dead silence, yet the five around his bag seemed to be conversing with great intensity.

The man on his right wore fairly modern clothing. The others wore ancient clothing as if from different times and places in history. The five men were lost in conversation and unaware that he was staring at them. He received the distinct impression that they were talking about him.

He watched them for a long time. The man on his left had a strained expression, and his face looked hard and beaten. He was the first to notice Charlie watching them. He started with surprise and alerted the others who also seemed surprised. Then the five men vanished, but the one who had been standing behind them stayed. He stood at Charlie's right, beside a dark horse. He projected an aura of blackness and returned Charlie's stare with powerful malice. He was a fearsome giant of a man dressed like an ancient warrior from the fifteenth or sixteenth century. His legs were bare at the thigh, but covered with armor from the knee down. Although his arms were bare, his chest was protected by an armored vest. He had a swarthy complexion and long curly hair which flowed out from under his helmet.

Charlie didn't dare take his eyes off this man, and they stared at each other for a time that seemed to last forever. Never had Charlie felt such hate emanate from another being. Finally the dark warrior sneered at Charlie and disappeared.

Charlie immediately crawled out of his sleeping bag and prayed. He told Heavenly Father what he'd experienced and expressed his fear. Then the Spirit comforted and warmed him throughout and reassured him that everything would be all right. He felt good again and was able to go back to sleep until morning broke.

Of the experience Charlie said, "Steve, as God is my witness, I was wide awake when I saw these people. I got out of my sleeping bag right after the dark man disappeared. I know they were talking about me!"

He spoke with a fervor I have to believe. He is as competent as any man I've known. I've never been able to discover any unsavory motive for telling the story. I thought he was closer to God spiritually than anyone I knew in the area at that time. I believed him then and I believe him now. During Thanksgiving of 1991, I visited him in Ogden and he reconfirmed the story. Charlie has a testimony based on experience that Satan and his forces are real and so is their interest in each one of us.

Satan not only opposes our journey on the path of faith to God, he also seeks to lead us down highways of skepticism. He teaches skepticism in the same way that he teaches us not to pray. "For the evil spirit teacheth not a man to pray, *but teacheth him that he must not pray*" (2 Ne. 32:8; emphasis mine).

One of my co-workers once said she sometimes felt an inner resistance to prayer, even though she knew that when she prayed her troubles flowed out and peace flowed in. Considering the remarkable rewards of prayer, I ask you, where else could this resistance come from? Reminding ourselves that Satan is real and does not want us to pray can rouse our determination to really talk with Heavenly Father.

Satan's resistance makes it difficult to travel on the path of faith, but that difficulty is part of the price we must pay to receive the blessings we desire. We need to persist in spite of it. President Kimball said that too many men "would have the harvest before the planting, the reward before the service, the miracle before the faith."[2] We would reach our destination before we begin our journey. The journey is difficult. Yet, for all its difficulty, there are extraordinary blessings for those who begin the climb. Don't be afraid. God will run to assist you. "The journey of a thousand miles begins with a single step."

The First Step Is Learning to Recognize Our Miracles

The first step is learning to recognize God's miracles. Wouldn't our Father be more inclined to give miracles to those who appreciate them? But we can't appreciate things we don't recognize. You may have no difficulty recognizing blessings or inspiration in your life, but you may have trouble seeing their miraculous nature. After reading some of the stories in the following chapters, you might be tempted to think, "That's not a miracle; that's inspiration and a blessing, but it's not a miracle." To change that thought, consider the relationship between blessings, inspiration, and miracles.

The Latin root for *miracle* is *miraculum,* which means "a strange thing;"[3] an act of God; something divine, surprising, inexplainable. Inspiration is "a divine influence upon human beings."[4] When we receive inspiration which produces surprising results, isn't that a miracle? Isn't it an inexplicable act of God producing surprising results? Inspiration might be the kind of miracle most often received, but it's still a miracle. To hear the voice of God is a miracle. I think a miracle is anything that happens because God intervenes in our lives.

When our Father blesses someone, he grants them a divine favor or gift,[5] such as greater physical strength or more powerful speaking ability, etc. To bless something also means to consecrate it and make it sacred or holy. When God blesses us, he also sanctifies or beautifies our lives in some way.[6] It's a "special benefit or favor."[7] But couldn't we say exactly the same things about miracles and inspiration? A blessing is also an act of God, often producing surprising and inexplicable results. Isn't that a miracle?

Why does God make miracles? Why does God inspire us? He creates miracles and grants inspiration to bless us. When we discover an act of God, doesn't it heighten our sense of the sacred? When we see God's work in our lives, aren't we comforted or gladdened? Doesn't God create each miracle or grant every inspiration to lift, assist, or ennoble us in some way? Isn't every miracle a blessing and isn't every blessing a miracle?

When God acts in my behalf to produce a "strange" event, then by definition, I have received a miracle, whether or not I recognize it as such. When God grants a request, he's made a miracle. When God creates something no one can match or explain, he's made a miracle.

When God denies a request, he can also be making a miracle. Recently a friend told me that he and his wife asked Heavenly Father whether she should return to work and take a good job which had been offered to her. They needed the money, but twice the Lord clearly said no. One month later they learned that she was going to have a baby. The wife did not return to work, but they have been helped financially to pay their bills. We can't always see the blessing, but the scriptures say that God "doeth not anything save it be for the benefit of the world" (2 Ne. 26:24). Wouldn't this always be true—even when our Father says no to our requests?

A miracle doesn't have to be dramatic. It can, in fact, be so simple that no one notices it at all. For example, eyesight is a blessing, but it is also a miracle, an act of God, a divine gift. It may not seem so at first because almost all people enjoy it, but can you explain it? Scientists can't. The *New York Times* reported that

> after two decades of research, [scientists] have yet to teach machines the seemingly simple act of being able to recognize everyday objects and to distinguish one from another.

Instead, they have developed a profound new respect for
the sophistication of human sight. . . . The human retina is the
envy of the computer scientists. Its 100 million rods and cones
and its layers of neurons perform at least 10 billion calculations
per second.[8]

The astronomer Robert Jastrow said, "The eye appears to have
been designed; no designer of telescopes could have done better."[9] Who, then, designed the human eye? It certainly was no
man. They're still stumped. It is surprising the scientists. Is it luck?
Is it explainable? Is it remarkable? I believe our eyesight is an
incredible miracle.

Life itself is a miracle. The basic cell needs 2,000 different
enzymes to sustain its life's activity. The chance for obtaining
these 2,000 enzymes by luck has been calculated by scientists to
be one chance in $10^{40,000}$.[10] This number is mind-boggling! As a
comparison, "it has been calculated that there are approximately
10^{65} atoms in a galaxy."[11] The scientific exponent of $10^{40,000}$ means
10 followed by 40,000 zeros. In order to print $10^{40,000}$ on a page
with sixty zeros on every line and forty lines on every page, we
would need almost seventeen pages. The astronomer Fred Hoyle
says that one chance in $10^{40,000}$ is "an outrageously small probability" that cannot be faced. He says that "this simple calculation
wipes the idea [of luck] entirely out of court."[12] These 2,000 different enzymes are just one of many miraculous steps essential for
life. If you think about it, life is an astounding miracle and blessing. Wiggle your little finger slowly and marvel. Explain how you
do that. Is it a blessing or a miracle, or both?

M. Scott Peck is a psychiatrist who wrote an explosively popu-
lar book about spiritual growth entitled *The Road Less Travelled*,
which has sold more than two million copies and continues to sell
incredible numbers in the bookstores. Scott Peck made the book
remarkable to me by devoting 127 pages to the role of religion and

miracles in spiritual growth. In his discussion he said, "Fifteen years ago, when I graduated from medical school, I was certain that there were no miracles. Today I am certain that miracles abound."[13]

He goes on to explain how his perception changed so dramatically. First he began to notice that a wide variety of commonplace events upon closer examination had a miraculous nature. He said, "This openness . . . then allowed me to begin routinely looking at ordinary existence with an eye for the miraculous. The more I looked, the more I found. If there were but one thing I could hope for from the reader of the remainder of this book, it would be that he or she possesses the capacity to perceive the miraculous."[14]

All miracles are generous acts of God to draw us closer to him. Any blessing from heaven is a miracle, and if you recognize it as such, God will be more likely to make more miracles for you. I search for miracles in sublime places because I believe God gives them to those who appreciate them. He has done and will do many more things for us as we recognize his miraculous hand in our lives.

A Second Step Is Recognizing Our Power to Choose Faith or Skepticism

Skepticism is a habit, but it is a habit we choose. Belief is also a choice and can become a habit just as skepticism can. Doubting Thomas refused to believe that Christ was resurrected and alive after the crucifixion, even though reliable witnesses reported Christ's appearance to him. He said, "Except I shall see in his hands the print of the nails, and put my finger into the print of the nails, and thrust my hand into his side, I will not believe" (John 20:25).

When Jesus appeared to the apostles in a room after his crucifixion, he said to Thomas, "Reach hither thy finger, and behold my hands; and reach hither thy hand, and thrust it into my side: and be not faithless, but believing" (vs. 27). Then Jesus added, "Thomas, because thou hast seen me, thou hast believed: blessed are they that have not seen, and yet have believed" (John 20:27, 29).

The statements of both Jesus and Thomas imply that faith or doubt is a choice. Why should Christ rebuke him if Thomas could not help his doubt? Thomas chose his doubt; therefore, Christ could reprove him. He knew Thomas could change his mind. Thomas chose to believe after seeing and touching Christ's wounds. Others chose to believe without such evidence, and they were more blessed. Why? Because their faith was greater. This choice of faith or skepticism is a conscious act of will in the beginning, but gradually becomes an unconscious habit—a habit which begins with a single thought, then grows into a web of feelings as habits do. We can form the habit of faith in the same way we may have formed the habit of doubt. We can begin with a single thought of faith and continue to add thoughts of faith until we have woven a new web of feelings which carry us to our Father.

A Third Step Is Learning to Control Our Thoughts

Faith and doubt are both feelings which are created by our thoughts. When we exercise our thoughts of faith, fear vanishes and we feel courage and strength to explore life's possibilities. The feeling of confidence increases within us and moves us forward to develop new skills and to participate in new experiences. Conversely, when we exercise our doubtful thoughts, courage vanishes and we feel anxious and worried about exploring life's possibilities. The feeling of fear increases within us and moves us to withdraw from opportunity. We tend to remain where we are because it seems safer than moving into new territories.

Our skepticism and faith are both unique, "thought-feeling" combinations. The more I study the research and compare it with my own experiences, the more I'm moved to conclude that our thoughts, which we have total freedom to choose, literally create our feelings.

In counseling sessions I help clients experience this link by having them try a personal experiment. I get out one or two of the biggest and heaviest books I can find (usually a couple of dictionaries). Then I ask a client to stand, close his eyes, and raise his arms until they are parallel with the floor. I then place the books on the back of his left hand and steady the books, but let the full weight rest on his hand. I ask the client to notice the weight and think of a happy occasion in his life. While thinking of a good experience, he will usually have no trouble holding the weight.

Then I ask him to remember a distressing or unhappy experience. I can usually tell when his thoughts shift because his arm drops a bit and then rises again. I ask if he can feel the weight change. Every client I have tried this with has been able to feel the books get heavier. Actually, the books don't get heavier—the arm just gets weaker. It has been weakened by the client's distressing or unhappy thoughts. As we explore this experience, my clients are able to see that their loss of physical strength occurs at the very moment they change their thoughts. That's how close and how strong the link is.

I also suggest that my clients imagine a walk away from friends at a campfire into the woods during the night. I say something like, "When the campfire is out of sight, imagine the sounds of a wild animal moving in the woods behind you near your path. You are fearful because it might be a dangerous animal. Imagine turning back to the campfire, but walking faster and faster as the threatening sounds draw nearer and nearer. Soon you are running to the campfire before the animal catches you. As you reach the campfire out of breath, your camp mates laughingly confide they have played a joke on you and there was no wild animal at all." As we discuss the experience, my clients see that their feelings changed instantaneously from fear and anxiety to embarrassment and anger when the scenes in their minds changed.

Simple but powerful thoughts create feelings and behaviors.

Think the thought, and our minds create an appropriate feeling. Our minds link appropriate feelings to our thoughts, so thoughts of fear create feelings and actions of fear; thoughts of faith create feelings of faith; and feelings of faith create actions of faith.

Just prior to 1980, a pilot study examined the effectiveness of a new treatment for clinically depressed people. The researchers chose patients "suffering from moderate to severe depressive episodes. The majority had failed to improve in spite of treatment with two or more therapists at other clinics. Three-quarters were suicidal at the time of their referral. The average patient had been troubled by chronic or intermittent depression for eight years."[15] Many of the patients felt their condition was utterly hopeless.

The patients were divided into two groups. One group of nineteen was taught to recognize and control their thinking. The second group of twenty-five received an anti-depressant drug. All of the patients were thoroughly evaluated for depression before their therapy and at regular intervals for a year following their treatment. The doctors who evaluated the patients were not the doctors who treated them. After twelve weeks of treatment, fifteen of the nineteen "thought" patients recovered completely from their depression. That is, nearly 79% of these patients were no longer unhappy. On the other hand, only five of the twenty-five patients treated with the drug recovered completely from their depression. That's only 20%. Think about those results. Changing the patient's thoughts was four times more effective than simply taking a drug.*

The first principle of this treatment is this: *"All* your moods are created by your 'cognitions,' or thoughts. . . . You *feel* the way you

---

*Author's note: I am not using this example to suggest any treatment for depression. I am only using this particular study to show the potential power of our thoughts. I am not suggesting that anti-depressant drugs are not important in the treatment of depression. The consensus of current research seems to suggest that the most effective treatment is a combination of both drug and thought therapy. Some research which has followed up on patients after they discontinued therapy does indicate that those who have had both resist relapse better than those using drugs alone.

do right now because of the *thoughts you are thinking at this moment*. . . . Your thought actually *creates* the emotion."[16] This treatment is called cognitive therapy, meaning "thought" therapy. To change your thoughts is a simple idea, but in a way, aren't we the sum of our thoughts? Even the scriptures illustrate this vital link between thoughts and feelings.

> For they knew not what to think; for when they beheld [thought about] those that had been delivered out of bondage they were filled with exceeding great joy.
>
> And again, when they thought of their brethren who had been slain by the Lamanites they were filled with sorrow, and even shed many tears of sorrow.
>
> And again, when they thought of the immediate goodness of God, and his power in delivering Alma and his brethren out of the hands of the Lamanites and of bondage, they did raise their voices and give thanks to God.
>
> And again, when they thought upon the Lamanites, who were their brethren, of their sinful and polluted state, they were filled with pain and anguish for the welfare of their souls. (Mosiah 25: 8–11)

Their feelings changed every time they shifted their thoughts. If each change of thought generates a concurrent shift of feeling, then don't we need to take a close look at each of our thoughts? Don't we need to look at our skeptical thoughts? Is there really a rational basis for them, or are they just habits? You can shift your thoughts from "it can't be done" to "it might be possible." This would be a significant move away from skepticism and toward faith. Then you could shift your thoughts from "it might be possible" to "it is possible." The greatest shift would be to move them to "it will be done if it is God's will."

This shifting won't be easy. The mind-set of skepticism has its own pleasures and rewards. It makes us feel knowing and sure. It enables us to judge people, events, and circumstances with a faulty brand of assurance. In this sense, skepticism removes some doubt and uncertainty from our lives. If we say to ourselves, "that could never happen," it eliminates the responsibility of working toward that goal or event. We no longer need to keep considering the option. Eliminating possibilities eliminates attending accountability. It takes the worry for certain events out of our control and makes us not responsible. It enables us to forget about the attendant work. Make no mistake, skepticism has its own rewards, even though it closes the door of opportunity for us.

A Fourth Step Is Challenging Our Skepticism

Our National Guard unit once camped near the top of a mountain almost 10,000 feet above sea level. We pitched our tents at the edge of a beautiful meadow. Half of our tent was on the meadow and the other half was in a forest. I was assigned to guard duty from 3:00 A.M. to 6:00 A.M. on the last morning. I watched the stars until daybreak and marveled at the mountain forest. While I pondered the majesty of our location, I thought of our Heavenly Father who created it all. There is something awesome about the Milky Way which makes us feel properly reverent. When contemplating the stars, it is easier to sense how little we know and then marvel and renew our faith in God, who said to Job:

> *Where wast thou when I laid the foundations of the earth?*
> *declare, if thou hast understanding. (Job 38:4)*

This question helped Job regain his perspective after a long period of suffering. It works for those who already sense the awesome power behind the incredible order of things. When looking at the stars, most of us find it hard to believe in "the lucky accident." I think most of us believe God created the earth, moon, and stars. Polls confirm it:

- Nine Americans in ten say they have never doubted the existence of God.
- Seven in ten believe in life after death.
- Eight in ten believe God still works miracles.
- Nine in ten say they pray.[17]

If you believe in the God who created this marvelous world, ask yourself whether it is consistent to believe he has withdrawn his interest in our lives. Could he create you in his image and then abandon you? Can we believe he would abandon any of his children? Is it consistent to believe that God worked miracles in the Old and New Testaments, that he has worked miracles for others, and then deny that he will work miracles for you?

Here is my suggestion. Go stand or sit out under the stars to remind yourself of your own belief in our Father who created it all. Remind yourself of the miraculous nature of the world. Remind yourself that God created men and women, plants and animals, land and water, etc. Remember that you believe that he sends or withholds the rain and that he made the stars, etc. Then ask yourself this question: "If I believe he can do and did do all of this for me, do I really believe he will do nothing more for me?" Then consider these verses:

> *And who shall say that Jesus Christ did not do many mighty miracles? And there were many mighty miracles wrought by the hands of the apostles.*
>
> *And if there were miracles wrought then, why has God ceased to be a God of miracles and yet be an unchangeable Being? And behold, I say unto you he changeth not; if so he would cease to be God; and he ceaseth not to be God, and is a God of miracles.*
>
> *And the reason why he ceaseth to do miracles among the children of men is because that they dwindle in unbelief, and depart from the right way, and know not the God in whom they should trust.*

> *Behold, I say unto you that whoso believeth in Christ,*
> *doubting nothing, whatsoever he shall ask the Father in the*
> *name of Christ it shall be granted him; and this promise is unto*
> *all, even unto the ends of the earth. (Morm. 9:18–21. See also*
> *Morm. 9:7–11.)*

Challenge your skepticism. Suppose your skepticism is just a mental rut? What if it simply exists because you've habitually practiced it? Maybe you've just spent more time being skeptical than you have developing your faith. If we believe God created all that we see, how can we believe he doesn't care? How can we believe he's lost his power or desire to help? How can we believe that God created the miracle of life on earth and then just stopped working in our behalf? Is he dead? Some people believe that, but do you?

A Fifth Step Is Exercising

If you must exercise to develop physical strength or talents, why shouldn't you need to exercise to develop your faith? Dr. Laurence Morehouse is a professor of exercise physiology and director of the Human Performance Laboratory at UCLA. He has written twelve books, and his textbook has been a standard in colleges and universities. NASA consulted with him to develop exercises to keep astronauts from wasting away in space. He said that "we know that a man who does nothing for a month will lose eighty percent of his physical condition."[18] If this is true for our physical strength, might it also be true for spiritual strength? If a month-long, effortless cruise through outer space will eliminate eighty percent of a man's physical condition, then what will the same kind of effortless cruise through life do to our faith? Christ told his best disciples that they didn't have faith equal to the grain of a mustard seed (Matt. 17:20; Luke 17:6). How could that happen? The conclusion is inescapable. We must exercise our faith to strengthen it.

I once read the story of a woman who had an ugly rash on her face which ruined her appearance. For sixteen years she had consulted dermatologists and tried everything they suggested to no avail. She began to exercise her faith by searching out every scripture on health, healing, and faith. She copied them and carried them everywhere. She pondered them at stoplights, during housework, and before sleep. And her faith began to grow until it was strong enough for her to ask God, with real confidence, to be healed. She visualized her skin as clear and soft, even though her rash continued. She also thanked the Lord, ahead of time, for being healed and continued until her rash began to fade and at last disappeared.[19]

I believe faith is as much a talent, gift, or strength as any other ability or strength. We can exercise the faith we have and strengthen it. The truth is that our faith weakens when we fail to exercise it until it seems to disappear. Part of our work is to do everything we can to strengthen our faith. We must pray for faith, search for faith, and exercise our faith through obedience to God.

A Sixth Step Is Working

Another part of our responsibility is to do everything we can to obtain our righteous desire. Although the journey of a thousand miles begins with a single step, it requires many steps after that and we must take them. God will meet us and help us along the way, but we must work for our requests. We are responsible to study out whatever would help us reach our goals and do our part.

A costume designer for the Hill Cumorah Pageant told how on numerous occasions the Lord miraculously provided material to complete projects when it wouldn't have been available through any other means. In fact, this sister commented, "Sometimes around here the materials grow on the shelves."

Still, this didn't excuse her from doing all she could. On one occasion when she knew she would be short material on a project, this sister prayed, confident that the Lord would provide as he had in the past, yet they still ran out of material. The Spirit then whispered to her, "You know how to get more of that fabric yourself," which was true. She realized she still had time and money left in the budget. This sister had resources to do it herself, and the Lord instructed her to do just that.[20] Our Father wants us to be resourceful and confident. He wants us to work with the gifts he's given us. Although we should look to heaven for help, we must not overlook our own gifts, resources, and talents.

God wants us to develop and grow. This can't be done without work. In the Garden of Eden, God cursed the ground for our sakes. Before casting Adam and Eve out of the Garden into their new world, he said, "Thorns also and thistles shall it bring forth to thee. . . . In the sweat of thy face shalt thou eat bread" (Gen. 3:18–19). He set up life this way for our sakes, not his.

He knows we need to work against resistance to grow. That's what weight training is all about. No weightlifter ever got stronger by lifting little marshmallows. A weightlifter develops his strength by lifting heavier and heavier sets of weights. Whenever he stops lifting regularly, his strength diminishes. His muscles actually need the resistance to grow and develop. The strongest weight lifters lift the heaviest weights. This principle is true for our minds also. Our intelligence and competence are developed by thinking. That's why Heavenly Father expects us to think before we ask.

Once Oliver Cowdery was given permission to translate characters from the gold plates. God told him to pray for that privilege, and he would receive according to his faith (D&C 8:11). When Oliver tried to translate the characters, however, he failed. Oliver asked why and God answered him this way:

> *Behold, you have not understood; you have supposed that I would give it unto you, when you took no thought save it was to ask me.*

*But, behold, I say unto you, that you must study it out in
your mind; then you must ask me if it be right. (D&C 9:7–8)*

What must you contribute to convince your Heavenly Father
that you are serious about your request? How can you convince
him that your desire is more than a mere wish? You show him the
strength of your desire by the amount of work you do for it, the
effort you make to strengthen your faith, and the effort you make
to reach your desire.

A Seventh Step Is Learning from the Miracles of Others

Read, ponder, and pray about the miracles of which others
have testified. Study the miracles of the scriptures and the miracles of modern life. Read the testimonies in "Mormon Journal" in
the *Ensign.* I also recommend *Guideposts.* Here, writers testify of
God's miraculous work in their lives. These people have differing
religious affiliations, and some had or have no religious affiliation
at all, yet God worked miracles for them according to their faith
in him. Try to read the few stories I have included in the next
chapter with an open mind. I have chosen some dramatic
accounts to share. You may find some of them hard to believe, but
ask yourself why. Do you think the witnesses are lying? Do you
think they are incompetent? Are you somehow better qualified
than they to interpret their experiences?

It is easier to stop being skeptical when we have experienced a
miracle for ourselves or when we trust the witness implicitly. It is
important to be discerning, but we must still remain believing and
open. To assure yourself that miracles are real, gather your own
faith-promoting experiences from the lives of people you know
are honest. If you are respectful, many people will share their
experiences with you. Take note of the personal stories of ward
members who share them in Sunday School, Relief Society, priesthood classes, sacrament meetings, or firesides. Seek these people

out later if you need clarification.

When I was a teenager, our ward needed money for our budget, which was some thousands of dollars in the red. Ward members needed to make an extra financial sacrifice to bring us out of debt. Our bishop, however, discerned that we would need the faith to pay it. So he asked us all to fast and pray before a special meeting at the church. Being young and hungry, I really did not pay attention to the speakers, except one—my father. Bishop Griffiths had asked him to share a personal experience with the ward members—a story I had never heard before.

It was a story about his miraculous experience with tithing. I knew my dad was a full tithe payer, but I had never known why. I was so deeply impressed with his sincerity that I could not dismiss his testimony.

His story isn't folklore to me. I believe it completely. I adopted his tithing policy and have experienced even more dramatic results. I trust my dad as the most honest man I know. His experience became mine. I could believe him because I knew he couldn't lie. Because he was closer to me (here and now) than Malachi (there and then), I was able to believe more easily and thus cross a chasm from his experience to my own experience.

Elder Ted E. Brewerton tells of a miracle recorded in his family's history. A hot loaf of bread, wrapped in a white cloth, appeared mysteriously for two hungry elders on a lonely road in New Zealand. One of these missionaries was James E. Fisher, Elder Brewerton's grandfather. These missionaries wrote home about this mysterious, hot loaf of bread wrapped in a white cloth. The next letter they received was from the wife of Elder Fisher's companion. She said that at the time they discovered their hot loaf of bread, she discovered one of her own bread pans was empty when she went to take it from the oven. She said that a white cloth on the kitchen table had also disappeared.[21]

Again, this story of the loaf of bread is not folklore for Elder Brewerton and his family.

My own great-great-great-grandfather, Benjamin Freeman Bird, and his sons were present when Brigham Young and Sidney Rigdon spoke to the Saints after Joseph Smith was martyred. Benjamin Freeman Bird and his family testified that they saw Brigham Young transformed to take on the appearance and sound of Joseph Smith, and this was a sign for them to follow Brigham Young West. That is why they came West. The transformation of Brigham Young isn't folklore in our family.

Stories from those who are close to us can be easier to believe and harder to dismiss. They start out being more real to us, and the more we ponder and consider them, the more we become open to them. Thus, our faith grows.

I imagine many of your neighbors have experienced miracles of one sort or another which they haven't shared with you. Part of the reason is that miraculous experiences are sacred, so people share them only on special occasions. Nevertheless, I've learned that people will share their stories if you approach them sincerely. Many of the stories in the next chapter were experiences people shared with me because I asked them. I gave them nothing but an opportunity to share with an interested person. I've used just a fraction of the many stories I've collected from other people. The Bible stories tell about them, there, and then, but this is *you, here,* and *now.* The stories in the following chapters, which have occurred more recently, narrow the chasm between the past and the present. Seeing that people today receive miracles can strengthen our belief that we, too, can receive miracles.

An Eighth Step Is Remembering Our Miracles

Heavenly Father makes miracles for those who love him. As Christ said, "Unto as many as received me gave I power to do many miracles" (D&C 45:8). I do not believe he works miracles to change the minds of skeptics, but rather he works miracles to bless his disciples. I also believe there are many living disciples who have received many miracles. Their testimonies are impressive but easily forgotten. So, when you hear of a miracle from a friend or ward member which touches your heart in some way, write it down. Record it in your journal, even if it is another person's experience. Whenever you experience something miraculous, write it down, remember it, and give thanks to God.

If the costume designer for the Hill Cumorah Pageant hadn't recorded her experiences, would you and I know anything about them? In her story she wrote: "Many times I have recorded in my journal instances in which it seemed clear that the hand of the Lord was with us. I'm grateful for these blessings and miracles, for they are beyond price."22 If miraculous experiences are truly beyond price to us, then why carelessly discard them by failing to record them? How will Heavenly Father feel about working more miracles for us if we fail to remember the ones he has already given? Moses warned the Israelites:

> *Beware that thou forget not the* LORD *thy God . . . Lest when thou hast eaten and art full, and hast built goodly houses, and dwelt therein . . . Then thine heart be lifted up, and thou forget the* LORD *. . . Who fed thee in the wilderness with manna . . . And thou say in thine heart, My power and the might of mine hand hath gotten me this wealth. (Deut. 8:11–17)*

Consider how easy it is to forget our miracles. Once my son Alan bore a tearful testimony of his gratitude to God and our family that our prayers had been answered and he was cured of a potentially crippling arthritis. But we forgot to write it down, and we didn't speak of it often amongst ourselves. Later, when his testimony was wavering, I reminded him of the experience. Then I discovered, much to my surprise and sorrow, that he couldn't remember all the prayers which had been miraculously answered in his behalf and which had occurred during a period of more than a year and a half of doctor and hospital visits, including physical therapy exercises and shots which were terribly painful to him.

The scriptures are loaded with directions for people to write down or record their experiences. Consider the Book of Mormon writers' difficult and tedious work engraving the metal plates. Yet if they and the Bible writers hadn't recorded their miracles and revelations, what would we have to build our faith on? Christ commanded the Nephites to "write the things which [they had] seen and heard" (3 Ne. 27:23). The Lord has also commanded us to keep a record of the spiritual things that we experience (D&C 21:1). How else can we remember? Nearly everything that is remembered in history has been written down. We write down vital information and then we review it regularly to fuse it into our soul. We forget so quickly unless we take pains to remind ourselves. S. Dilworth Young said that the palest ink is stronger than the finest memory.

A Ninth Step Is Teaching These Principles to Others

There is one other marvelous way to remember our blessings. That is to testify of them to others when appropriate. Sunday School classes or family home evenings are perfect places to do this. Jesus said to Peter, "And when thou art converted, strengthen thy brethren" (Luke 22:32). This is simply helping others find the Lord by sharing your own experiences with them as directed by the Spirit. Christ commanded his disciples to "teach the things which [I have] expounded unto [you]" (3 Ne. 23:14). Our Heavenly Father knows that we'll remember better the things that we teach to someone else. Once I asked a quorum member to teach one of the priesthood lessons in our elders meeting. At the end of his lesson he thanked me and said, "I learned more than I ever did before." So share your experiences with your spouse. Testify of God's hand in your life to your children. Humbly tell your Sunday School class about the blessings you have received and encourage them to seek their own. In the *Lectures on Faith,* we are told

> how it was that God became an object of faith . . . and we have seen that it was human testimony, and human testimony only that excited this inquiry. . . . It was the credence they gave to the testimony of their fathers, this testimony having aroused their minds to inquire after the knowledge of God; the inquiry frequently terminated, indeed always terminated when rightly pursued, in the most glorious discoveries and eternal certainty.[23]

In this book, I chose witnesses which helped me remember God's miracles, and I wrote them down to share with you. The experience has affected me powerfully. Yet, I also did it to show what kinds of miracles are possible. Taken individually, each step will help build our faith to some degree, but I think that our faith will really grow after we have taken all of these steps and whatever other steps God may so direct us to take. These steps may challenge us, but I believe the result is surely worth the effort, for Christ has said:

> *If ye will have faith in me ye shall have power to do what-soever thing is expedient in me. . . .*
> *And now, my beloved brethren . . . has the day of miracles ceased?*
> *Or have angels ceased to appear unto the children of men? Or has he withheld the power of the Holy Ghost from them? Or will he, so long as time shall last. . . .*
> *Behold I say unto you, Nay; for it is by faith that miracles are wrought; and it is by faith that angels appear and minister*

unto men; wherefore, if these things have ceased wo be unto the children of men, for it is because of unbelief. (Moro. 7:33, 35–37)

Would you like divine help to develop love and unity in your family? Would you like a closer relationship with your wife or husband? Do you have a rebellious child you would like to return lovingly to your arms? Would you like more satisfaction in your job or career? Would you like to marry happily? Do you want to love your spouse more or understand your children better? Would you like more guidance in your work or church calling? I believe these are all things we can realistically seek and hope for, provided we approach our Heavenly Father in the manner he has directed in his scriptures, remember free agency, and always seek his will. Reviewing chapters two through six will help us remember those precious steps leading to communion with God.

Notes

1. *Lectures on Faith* (Salt Lake City: Deseret Book, 1985), 5.
2. Spencer W. Kimball, *Faith Precedes the Miracle* (Salt Lake City: Deseret Book, 1974), 4.
3. David B. Guralnik, ed. *Webster's New World Dictionary of the American Language,* 2nd college ed. (Cleveland: William Collins & World Publishing Co., Inc., 1974), 907.
4. Ibid., 729.
5. Ibid., 150.
6. J.I. Rodale, *The Synonym Finder* (Emmaus, PA: Rodale Press, 1978), 120.
7. *Webster's New World Dictionary,* 150.
8. *New York Times,* "Computer Scientists Stymied in Their Quest to Match Human Vision," by William J. Broad, September 25, 1984, p. C1.
9. Robert Jastrow, *The Enchanted Loom: Mind in the Universe* (New York: Simon and Schuster, 1981), 96.
10. Fred Hoyle & N.C. Wickramasinghe, *Evolution from Space* (New York: Simon and Schuster, 1981), 24.

11. Percival Davis, Dean H. Kenyon, and Charles B. Thaxton, *Of Pandas and People* (Dallas, Texas: Haughton Publishing Co., 1993), 146.

12. Hoyle, 24.

13. M. Scott Peck, M.D., *The Road Less Travelled: A New Psychology of Love, Traditional Values and Spiritual Growth* (New York: A Touchstone Book, 1978), 229; emphasis mine.

14. Ibid., 230.

15. David D. Burns, *Feeling Good: The New Mood Therapy* (New York: New American Library, 1980), 14.

16. Ibid., 11–12.

17. Gary Wills, "The Things That Matter," *Reader's Digest*, May 1991, 84.

18. Laurence E. Morehouse and Leonard Gross, *Total Fitness: in 30 Minutes a Week* (New York: Simon and Schuster, 1975), 9–10, 26.

19. Norman Vincent Peal, *Positive Imaging: The Powerful Way to Change Your Life* (New York: Fawcett Crest, 1982), 136–37.

20. Gail Argetsinger, "Costumes and Small Miracles," *Ensign*, July 1985, 22–24.

21. Ted E. Brewerton, "Miracles," *New Era*, November 1990, 4–7.

22. Argetsinger, 22.

23. *Lectures on Faith,* 24.

8

The Blessings of Faith in God

God will provide our daily bread.

When Jesus prayed, "Give us this day our daily bread," he showed us God's interest in our daily physical welfare, our economic well-being, our jobs. In the beginning, he created the earth and placed animals, herb yielding seed, and trees yielding fruit to be our meat (see Gen. 1:25, 29). Then he created us in his image and gave us dominion over all the earth (Gen. 1:26). And when Adam and Eve left the Garden of Eden, the Lord made them coats of skins to protect them from the elements (Gen. 3:21). "For, behold, the beasts of the field and the fowls of the air, and that which cometh of the earth, is ordained for the use of man for food and for raiment, and that he might have in abundance" (D&C 49:19). Alma tells us to "cry unto him over the crops of your fields" (Alma 34:25). Still, there are two important principles which have a bearing on God's providence.

The first principle is that our Heavenly Father hates greed. Grasping for the earth's riches can cost us the "riches of eternity."

President Kimball told about some men who went into a jungle with new traps to catch monkeys—boxes with small holes bored in the top just large enough for a monkey to slip a paw into. They put the monkeys' favorite nut into the boxes, placed the boxes under the trees, and disappeared. When the monkeys came down from the trees to check out the boxes, they saw the nuts inside and reached in to grab them. They soon found they couldn't get the nuts out because their paws, balled into little fists wrapped tightly around the nuts, would not fit back through the tiny holes in the tops of the boxes.

While the monkeys had their paws stuck in the boxes, the men came "out of the underbrush [to] converge on the monkeys." President Kimball said, "Here is the curious thing: When the monkeys saw the men coming, they would shriek and scramble about with the thought of escaping; but as easy as it would have been, they would not let go of the nut so that they could withdraw their hands from the boxes and thus escape. The men captured them easily." The monkeys lost their freedom because of their own greed.[1]

Satan also uses greed to capture souls. As the Lord said, "What is a man profited, if he shall gain the whole world, and lose his own soul? or what shall a man give in exchange for his soul?" (Matt. 16:26). "But wo unto the rich, who are rich as to the things of the world. . . . and their hearts are set upon their treasures; wherefore, their treasure is their god. And behold, their treasure shall perish with them also" (2 Ne. 9:30). "Seek not for riches" (D&C 6:7; 11:7: 38:39; 2 Ne. 2:18; Alma 39:14). "I, the Lord, am not well pleased with the inhabitants of Zion . . . [for] their eyes are full of greediness. These things ought not to be and must be done away" (D&C 68:31–32).

I believe God wants us to live wisely and well, but he is not particularly interested in making us rich. He doesn't want us to put ourselves above our brothers and sisters, but instead commands us to "look to the poor and the needy, and administer to their relief that they shall not suffer" (D&C 38:35). Heavenly Father wants us to esteem our brothers as ourselves and have charity which "envieth not" (D&C 38:24; 1 Cor. 13:4; Moro. 7:45). The Lord has emphasized that "it is not given that one man should possess that which is above another" (D&C 49:19–20). A righteous father would care about all his children equally and not put one above another.

The second principle is that the windows of heaven are linked to the principle of tithing. "Bring ye all the tithes to the storehouse that there may be meat in mine house, and prove me now herewith, saith the Lord of hosts, if I will not open you the windows of heaven, and pour you out a blessing, that there shall not be room enough to receive it" (Mal. 3:10).

In the spring of 1978, I left the Army and returned to Utah to finish college. I needed money to register for school so I could qualify for benefits under the G.I. Bill, but I was unemployed, our savings had run out, and our family was without funds.

After discussing the situation with my wife, we prayed earnestly and asked Heavenly Father to help us, reminding him that we had always paid our tithing. The next day I received a call from a friend to whom I had loaned $2,400 five years before. He had made no payments, and the loan was three years overdue. I had written it off as a complete loss. My friend said that he and his wife had driven down from Tacoma, Washington, to Utah to pay me off with interest. With that money I was able to register at Weber State College and cover our basic living expenses until I could secure a job and financial grants for school expenses. Peggy and I both know Heavenly Father sent that money at that time to take care of our needs. I believe that if I pay my tithing in faith with rejoicing, and am managing my life in a responsible and provident way, then I can pray with confidence for my Father's assistance in providing for my family.

Dr. Norman Vincent Peale tells how tithing helped him and his wife, Ruth, get through some tough times during the Great Depression of the 1930s. Although he is not LDS, his experiment with the Lord's scriptural promise worked just the same as it did for my father and myself. Dr. Peale—pastor to one of the largest congregations in New York, author of at least fourteen books, and former publisher of *Guideposts* magazine—said he "recommended tithing to thousands of people, and hundreds have been persuaded to try it. Of those hundreds, not one has ever come back to me and said that the experiment failed, or that he regretted it, or that it was a mistake. Not a single one."[2]

Sometimes our Father gives money or other necessities directly to his children in miraculous ways. While on a mission, Heber C. Kimball once took a stage with Brigham Young to return to Kirtland, Ohio. They kept their money in a wallet in their trunk, and when they left Pleasant Garden they had $13.50. Their passage to Indianapolis took almost all of their money, yet when they arrived, they found enough money in their wallet for fare to Richmond, Indiana. At Richmond, Heber found sufficient funds in the wallet to get them to Dayton. There, they spent the night, and when Brigham went to the trunk he found enough money to get them to Columbus, where they spent the next night. At Columbus, he had enough money to get them to Worcester. There, Brigham found money in the trunk to cover his expenses and buy two tickets to Cleveland. They continued in this manner to Kirtland, where they added up their expenses and found they had paid more than $87.00 in travel fares and expenses from the original $13.50.[3]

Lest you think these things only happen to prophets, consider the following story that happened to a family in England during World War II. Two years after the war, they were still on rations in the coldest town in England. It had snowed for six weeks, and the snowdrifts were above their heads. No coal cart could reach their home, and when they used the last of their coal they were afraid they would freeze to death.

Kneeling in prayer, they asked the Lord to help them. A sense of peace displaced their fear, and they retired to bed, content to leave the matter with Heavenly Father.

During that week every single day the mother found a little pile of coal in the same corner she had left empty the day before. The entire family marveled that the little pile of coal lasted through the evening and kept them warm. This little miracle reoccurred daily until her husband was able to get all the coal they needed on Saturday.

This mother later wrote, "I still have no explanation for this incident. All I know is that it did happen and six of us witnessed it. And we know that God lives and answers prayers."[4] Think of the wonder of it! Six people verify the circumstances of this miracle, and an entire family was blessed. This is only one example; I have other stories like this in my personal files, and you may know of others, too. Now let's consider some other ways the Lord helps his children meet their temporal needs.

Our Heavenly Father often helps his children find work. After leaving the Naval Chaplain Corps, I found it very difficult to get a job and had been unemployed for nearly three months. Our funds were running low, and our monthly expenses were very high. Peggy and I had been praying all along, but we humbled ourselves by fasting while we went to the Oakland Temple. We put our names on the prayer roll there, so others could pray for us also. During our session in the temple, Peggy and I both felt reassured that I would be offered a position soon.

We had been asked to introduce ourselves and speak that following Sunday in sacrament meeting. Though she hadn't planned to do so, Peggy mentioned in her talk that I was looking for work. Right after the meeting, a man said he felt impressed to discuss a position with me. When we met later I learned that he felt the need for a personnel manager, a position he had never before filled. The night we spoke, he asked what salary I would need to support my wife. I told him, and he offered me the position for that amount. I had never been a personnel manager before and he had never used one before, but it worked out well for both of us.

Heavenly Father will also help his children accomplish their work more effectively. Some time ago I read about a young man who needed money to serve the Lord on a mission. Thousands of workers on strike were competing for construction jobs like his. It was vital to his dream to keep his job, but he had experienced angry harassment from his boss about his desire to serve a mission.

The young man was sent to work on a guardrail that was uprooted from the ground and which had thirteen legs of steel extending from it like teeth in a gigantic comb. A block of cement, the size of a barrel, encased each steel leg, and his boss had told him to knock the cement off the legs.

The work was exhausting. The stunning reverberations in the sledgehammer numbed his shoulders and arms. He knew he had reached his limit when he had broken off only one small chunk, yet he only had till noon to show his boss some results or he'd be unemployed again.

Resting his hammer on the ground and struggling to compose his emotions, he reminded Heavenly Father that he didn't want to earn money to buy a fancy car, but to serve a mission. Immediately a lucid and powerful thought came forcefully to his mind: "Instead of striking the cement, strike the steel."

Still not understanding why, he brought the hammer down forcibly several times on the steel next to the cement block and watched the cement crack into chunks which dropped away from the posts. With renewed strength, he cleared the guardrails in less than two hours, and the results left his boss standing in stunned silence. The next morning his boss greeted him with new respect, gave him work for as long as he wanted, and never, in his presence, uttered another disparaging remark about the Church or his plans for a mission.[5]

I believe the Lord can work just such miracles with all of us in our work each day. He can help us in our current project or undertaking.

During my first year of college, Freshman Composition 102 required more work than any other class I had ever taken. The endless footnote and bibliographic requirements bewildered me and so I avoided the work. I didn't read the textbook or take any notes. I didn't choose a topic or do any research, and inevitably, when the deadline arrived, I had nothing to turn in. So I skipped the last week of class and the final exam, and predictably, I received an F.

Five years later, I joined the Army to work as a North Vietnamese linguist, and the Army assigned me to Ramasun Station in northern Thailand. A college instructor came to our post two evenings each week, so I enrolled in Freshman Composition again. I took the first assignment to the barracks and lay on my bunk staring at it. I just couldn't think of anything to write. During the next four nights I continued to hope for some ideas, but none came. Fearing another failure, I officially withdrew from the class.

When I left the Army and returned to college, I knew I had to complete this class in order to graduate, but my poor academic record discouraged me and I avoided Freshman Composition 102. That term, I dropped two of my three classes to avoid failing them, for I knew the college would not allow me to continue if I failed any more classes. During this time I often thought of withdrawing from school and seriously discussed it with my wife for two weeks before I finally resolved to pray about it. I clearly needed some sort of divine help to graduate from college.

One afternoon, I closed my bedroom door and knelt down to pray. I had no idea what my Heavenly Father would say, but I was determined to find out. I spent quite some time listening on my knees; finally a powerful thought entered my mind: *Steve, stay in school. Do your best and I will help you.*

The impression clearly came from Heavenly Father, filling my mind and heart with warmth and strength. With this assurance that the Lord would help me finish school, I registered the next term for Freshman Composition 102. I began by finding a topic I liked and doing a lot of library research. I accumulated an impressive file of material as the deadline drew ever closer, but I put off the actual writing until the weekend before the paper was due. That Friday night I tried to write, but my thoughts were confused and I couldn't get anything on paper. I knelt again in fervent prayer and asked, "Why can't I write?"

I dumped out my frustration and pleaded for help. I couldn't understand why this was happening again because this time I was prepared. I had listened to the teacher and had taken notes in class. I had read the textbook and done some tremendous research. Why wouldn't any words come? I waited and listened.

Some time passed, but I kept listening. Then quiet words and a warm feeling reassured me: *Everything will be all right. I will meet you at the library tomorrow when it opens. Go to bed now and get some rest.*

Early the next morning, I went straight to the library. When it opened I found a quiet study carrel in the back. I spread out my papers and began to examine them, but I still had no idea how to begin. I read through my notes again, becoming more frustrated because I didn't know what to write. I had expected help from Heavenly Father, but I felt more alone than ever. Bowing my head, I asked, "Heavenly Father, where art thou?"'

After a pause, there came a quiet response: *I was waiting for you to look for me. How can I help you?*

The mild reproof humbled me, and I hesitated before answering, "I'm stuck. I don't know what to write, and yet this paper is vital. I've got to write it to pass the class and graduate."

As I continued to pray and as I pondered the consequences of failing, I grew more humble and fought back my tears. It hurt to stare at the possibility of failure once again. As I slipped into deeper humility, I heard clear words form in my mind: *Listen carefully and I will show you how to write this paper.*

Then I felt his love fill my soul and a light came on in my mind. I knew what to write. I knew what the theme would be. I knew what ideas to propose and how to use my sources to logically defend them. Heavenly Father helped me outline the entire paper clearly in my mind. I began to write as fast as I could. Yet even at top speed, I couldn't write as fast as the ideas came. I had to stop occasionally just to rest my hurting hand, and yet the words continued to roll through my mind. Time stood still while I wrote furiously. Heavenly Father repeatedly led me back into my research notes for supporting quotations, and I wrote until I was exhausted. My hand throbbed, my back hurt, and I finally said, "Heavenly Father, I can see how the paper has to be finished and I have most of the rough draft done. I need to type the final report today because tomorrow is the Sabbath and the paper is due Monday morning. I'm going home now, but please let thy Spirit help me remember the things that thou hast shown me."

I had been in the library almost five hours and it had seemed like five minutes. At home I learned how hard it is to reference footnotes and compile a bibliography, but I finished my paper at four o'clock the next morning. I could hardly wait for Monday to come so I could turn it in.

I really wasn't surprised to see the A my teacher gave me. From that point on I knew Heavenly Father was interested in every aspect of my life. As a result of this experience, I began to pray over each college assignment, and I grew more successful and confident as I prayed. Divine help poured down from heaven as I humbled myself before the Lord. Without the Lord's help, I had flunked nearly half of my classes in a term, received an official academic warning, and failed to earn a single A in college. With the Lord's help I graduated with honors.

I know our Father is willing to help us in our work and that it is well worth our time to ask him. He can soften the hearts of those in authority over us; he can soften our hearts toward them; or he can strengthen us to bear up under a difficult situation until a change can be made. He can guide our daily decisions. He can help us choose our careers and help us prepare for them if we are in that stage of our lives. He can help us appreciate the work we have and help us work with greater effectiveness. I have even read the journal of a miner for whom God moved a dangerous twenty-five-ton ledge of rock.

God has the power to heal us.

Our Savior's heart flowed with compassion for the sick. This is a trait that marks his character. Of all the miracles he performed, healing was the most frequent. When Christ visited his children in America he asked them, "Have ye any that are sick among you? . . . Have ye any that are lame, or blind, or halt, or maimed, or leprous, or that are withered, or that are deaf, or that are afflicted in any manner? Bring them hither and I will heal them, for I have compassion upon you; my bowels are filled with mercy . . . [and] I see that your faith is sufficient that I should heal you" (3 Ne. 17:7–8).

These words are a lesson to us on the importance of faith, for even though Jesus' bowels were "filled with compassion" towards these people, he could not or would not heal them until he saw that their faith was sufficient. When Jesus returned to his hometown, his neighbors still saw him as "the carpenter's son" and they could not believe in him. Therefore, the scripture says, "he did not many mighty works there because of their unbelief" (Matt. 13:54–58).

The apostle James said that when someone is sick we should "call for the elders of the church; and let them pray over him, anointing him with oil in the name of the Lord: And the prayer of faith shall save the sick" (James 5:14–15). Other scriptures remind us that healing, as all else, is conditional not only on our faith, but on God's will. Still, our faith is an essential element.

Combine hope with faith and the powers of God and if we are not appointed unto death, we can be healed of even the most dreaded conditions. During my mission I met a member whom I came to respect deeply, and I ate dinner in his home many times. During our dinner he told me that in the summer of 1960, eight years before I met him, he had taken the missionary discussions with his father. He was eighteen years old and had made no commitments then to join the Church, but from his experience with the missionaries, he decided to attend Dixie College in St. George, Utah. There, a roommate's example moved him to take the discussions again. He was impressed by the lessons, but not convinced. The next year he developed a serious relationship with a girl, but he knew she would only marry him in the temple. That's why he took a closer look at the Church for a third time. By the end of the school year, he knew the Church was true and asked to be baptized. But his baptism was delayed. He told me this story:

> On August 17, 1963, I had a car accident south of Cedar City, Utah. I hit a guardrail . . . and it came through the grill, split the engine, then found me. My brother was asleep in the backseat and never knew what hit him. . . .
>
> I can't say the same for me. I broke my right leg in five places, my right hip in seven places, broke eight ribs, my back in two places, my right arm in seventeen places, collapsed my right lung and ruptured my right kidney. I was paralyzed from my waist down.

They took me to St. George in a station wagon. They X-rayed me there and decided there wasn't anything they could do for me there, so they gave me some blood and saline . . . and sent me to Salt Lake in a station wagon.

That was a trip I don't want to repeat. First they took me to the wrong hospital and unloaded me, then loaded me back up, and off we went again to the Holy Cross this time because I was still a Catholic, I guess.

The doctor was there waiting for me, and I talked to him for about five minutes. I don't remember anything about the next twelve hours. I was in surgery for eight hours. He fixed my leg, hip, arm, and ribs. He left my back, lung, and kidney to fix later, if I lived long enough to fix them.

When I woke up, Mom and Dad were there. I don't remember much about the next two days except pain, a [Catholic] priest, a nurse, and my parents.

On the third day in intensive care *I asked my dad for the elders,* and he didn't know what I was talking about so the [Catholic] priest explained it to them. So up came the elders, who I am sure were sent from God to me.

They blessed me, and from the moment they took their hands from my head, my back was no longer broken. There was a stitched and bandaged wound from my ear to my Adam's apple that was gone [stitches and bandages were gone too].

During all the commotion the elders left, never to be heard from again. My doctor, the priest, and my parents were present during this time and all witnessed the change in me.

The doctor . . . had me X-rayed, and there was no sign of any back injury. I have seen three sets of X-rays, one from St. George (back broken), one from Salt Lake (back broken), and the third from Salt Lake (back not broken, no scar tissue).

My doctor had first estimated that I would be in the hospital ten months, if I lived. I was at home in six weeks. I was in a body cast, but I was home. I was out of my cast for Christmas and walking by the end of January. I was baptized on the 31st of January 1964. I was married in the St. George Temple on

March 12, 1965, and I have lived happily ever after. Can anyone ever see how I could ever become inactive when I owe the Lord so much?[6]

This friend later told me that he has been through the temple on behalf of his brother, who he is sure has accepted the gospel. He also told me that when he was released from the hospital, the doctor cut his bill in half because he felt his surgery had not been the reason for his recovery.

The second principle is that with enough faith, the Lord will heal us *if* he has no reason to refrain. "And again, it shall come to pass that he that hath faith in me to be healed, and *is not appointed unto death,* shall be healed" (D&C 42:48–51; emphasis mine). Scriptural examples do show that God has his own purposes, and these may affect his decision of *when* to heal or even *whether* to heal. Lazarus, the brother of Martha and Mary, fell sick. So they sent word of his illness to Jesus. And "when Jesus heard that, he said, This sickness is *not unto death,* but for the glory of God" (John 11:4; emphasis mine). The family and friends of Lazarus had to wait several days to establish the fact of Lazarus's death and of Christ's power over death. Nevertheless, when the time was right, when God and Christ's purposes were fulfilled, Jesus brought Lazarus forth from the tomb, "bound hand and foot with graveclothes" (John 11:43–45).

God may not heal us or may delay healing us for other reasons. In the scriptural example of Job, we see the Lord allow a righteous man to suffer, rather than heal him right away. Our Father asks Satan, "Hast thou considered my servant Job, that there is none like him in the earth, a perfect and an upright man, one that feareth God, and escheweth evil?" (Job 1:8). To *eschew* means to fear and shun something. In this case, Job shunned evil. Men just don't get any more righteous than that, and God said so himself. Job, who loved God, was allowed to suffer terribly. If Job did, in fact, pray for the safety, health, and preservation of his family, God did not grant his request. Nor did God move quickly to remove Job's personal, physical suffering even though our Father held Job in great esteem. Even at the end, God does not tell Job why he allowed such afflictions to befall him.

While it is true that Heavenly Father won't always heal us, I believe we should still seek healing from him during times of serious illness until we know the Lord's will. For one thing, we usually don't know when our allotted time is up, and so we should press ahead as though we still have a lot of living left to do and a lot of our mission yet to accomplish. It is a serious mistake to erroneously assume that we know it is time for our death, when in fact we simply may be lacking sufficient faith to be healed.

The same would be true for suffering. I believe it is a mistake to assume that our Heavenly Father is deliberately allowing us to suffer to fulfill some sort of divine purpose unless he has made that known to us in prayer. I believe it is generally wiser to assume that if our faith is sufficient the Lord will respond. If we are unsure, in our prayers we need to learn what our Heavenly Father wants for us. Paul asked for healing until he was told to drop his request (2 Cor. 12:7–9). If we are living close to our Father in Heaven we can trust that he will tell us when a request is not in accordance with his will.

The principle of agency implies responsibility for our choices. Our health choices always create consequences. In healing, we certainly have a responsibility to live in accordance with revealed health laws, such as the Word of Wisdom (D&C 89).

When the Lord says "seek and ye shall find," he may be saying we need to take more responsibility—do some research about our own health condition, seek more guidance, be willing to make more changes.

We should seek guidance from heaven as well as guidance from health specialists in all fields. In our prayers we might be led to certain practitioners who have the knowledge to help us. We might even be led to significant help from credible practitioners in holistic fields of medicine.

It is always good to talk with our Father about our health. Even one's time of death can sometimes be set back. When the righteous King Hezekiah was sick unto death, he asked the Lord to extend his life. Out of respect for Hezekiah's righteousness, the Lord granted the king's request and gave him another fifteen years of life. Then, the Lord gave Hezekiah a sign to assure him by turning back the shadow on the king's sundial ten degrees (2 Kgs. 20:1–11).

God will preserve us.

Our Father's concern extends to preserving our lives from danger. A good example of this would be the way in which he preserved Joseph when his brothers sold him into slavery in Egypt and then used Joseph to preserve Jacob's family—including his brothers. Joseph told his brothers when they came for food during the famine, "God did send me before you to preserve life" (Gen. 45:5). Generally, God's special preservation is reserved for the righteous. Moses said that God asked us to fear him and keep his commandments "that he might preserve us alive" (Deut. 6:24). In a psalm, David said that "the LORD preserveth all them that love him" (Ps. 145:20), and Nephi taught that God "will preserve the righteous by his power" (1 Ne. 22:17). Although not stated explicitly, this is only true until our appointed time of death and if we exercise sufficient faith (D&C 42:48).

Sometimes God gives us warnings, and we just plain have to listen to them. Bill Smith was my high priests group leader. A couple of years ago, he and a fellow worker were doing concrete work on the Flaming Gorge Dam. It is a concrete dam, 502 feet tall, blocking a river in a narrow canyon.

Bill and his partner were working at the bottom of a shaft, near the spillways. A platform had been rigged to run up and down the shaft, which extended from the top down to the bottom of the dam. Although Bill had been making his preparations for several days, for one reason or another he had been frustrated in his efforts to pour concrete in that shaft.

On the third day he was determined to go and get that concrete poured, but while he and his partner were at the bottom of the shaft, Bill had a strong feeling that they should get out of there. He shrugged it off, but the feeling returned, and he told his partner to come with him to the top.

When they got to the top the foreman rushed to meet them. His face was pale and he hurriedly explained that he thought Bill and his partner had been crushed at the bottom of the shaft. The electric winch holding the platform had inexplicably started in reverse and began to pull the platform back up the shaft. The winch would not shut down when workmen repeatedly pressed the "Off" button. While it was rising up the shaft, the platform had caught under some rebar. Several men riding the platform climbed off onto the rebar before the cable snapped. One fell with the platform to the bottom of the shaft and was killed.

The platform landed on Bill's concrete pouring equipment, the exact spot where Bill and his partner had been working just a few minutes earlier. Had Bill shrugged off his impressions and stayed where he was to pour concrete, he and his partner would have been killed.

The consequences for failing to listen to and obey spiritual warnings can be terrible. In 1852, William Dunbar went down to inspect the hold of a Missouri riverboat called the *Saluda*. He and Duncan Campbell were considering whether to buy tickets for ninety Latter-day Saints to leave St. Louis. William Dunbar said that when they entered the hold they both received the impression that some dreadful fate awaited the ship. Dunbar said when they looked at each other they both had tears streaming down their faces. A missionary, Elder Abraham O. Smoot, also felt a spiritual warning. Even when offered free passage on the *Saluda*, he refused to board.

Unfortunately, Dunbar and Campbell did not heed their warning and proceeded to make travel arrangements aboard the *Saluda* for themselves and the other Saints. After the boilers on the ship exploded, Dunbar regained consciousness on the riverbank with drenched clothes and a bloodied head. He soon found the body of his one-year-old son and later went to a temporary hospital where he watched his wife pass away. He found his five-year-old daughter while searching among the dead. That single terrible moment had taken his entire family. Looking back he remembered the spiritual message that would have saved his family. To the end of his days, he would lament the fact that he had ignored the Lord's warning.[7]

When we heed such spiritual promptings, we may never know what trouble we've avoided. President Harold B. Lee told of being warned as a boy not to go into a certain place. When he was asked what danger had lain therein, he replied that he didn't know because he didn't go in. William Dunbar tragically discovered what he was being warned against because he disregarded the warnings.

We need not only worthiness to receive such promptings but also sufficient sensitivity to recognize and have confidence in them. There are times when our Heavenly Father acts rather than speaks. I once read the story of an eighteen-year-old who herded sheep in eastern Idaho. One day he was sent to another camp which was a two-day journey by horseback. He was returning from his trip and was riding down a steep ravine when the trail collapsed and he and the horse slid down into a small stream. His horse ended up in a little sump of water on its backside with its feet sticking up into the air. The horse struggled valiantly to free itself, but each desperate effort only seemed to settle the horse more deeply in the muddy bog. It was no use. His horse was utterly helpless.

He knelt to pray, talking freely with the Lord, explaining his predicament, but saw no results. His apprehensions rose as the skylight dimmed, and he prayed again, remembering hearing of missionaries who said they had prayed long hours before getting help. Finally, mustering all his faith and humbling himself deeply, he asked again for guidance or help. He feared his horse would not survive the night in its contorted position, and he told the Lord in a very sincere but firm way how much he cared for its welfare.

On rising from his prayer, he was stunned. For there, standing on top of the steep bank they had slid down, was his horse— unhurt and unmoving!

His gratitude was unbounded. No horse could extricate itself from such a position, then climb a bank that an eighteen-year-old youth could not climb. This young man liked to think that an unseen personage miraculously rescued, then held his horse for him.[8]

God will heal our hearts.

Our Heavenly Father loves to see happy families and strong friendships. Although healing broken relationships is probably his most subtle miracle, it is possibly his most important. Our Savior said: "This is my commandment, That ye love one another, as I have loved you" (John 15:12). If we are to become like him, we have to learn to love one another as he loved us. Because he loves each of his children, I think he loves to answer yes when we request healing for broken hearts. I think he looks for reasons to restore our love and respect for one another.

Surely he has power to change our hearts. Isn't he the one who "knoweth the secrets of the heart" (Ps. 44:21)? Jesus said, "God knoweth your hearts" (Luke 16:15); he "searcheth the hearts" (Rom. 8:27) and is the "discerner of the thoughts and intents of the heart" (Heb. 4:12). Just look at a few examples from scripture. Heavenly Father "healeth the broken in heart" (Ps. 147:3). In referring to his children God said, "And I will give them one heart, and I will put a new spirit within you; and I will take the stony heart out of their flesh, and will give them an heart of flesh" (Ezek. 11:19). Alma once referred to a time when God had helped some Nephites by saying simply, "He changed their hearts" (Alma 5:7). The Lord softened "the heart of Ishmael, and also his household, insomuch that they did take their journey with us down into the wilderness to the tent of our father" (1 Ne. 7:5).

However, results are much more likely when we ask the Lord in our prayers to soften and heal our own hearts rather than someone else's because he has given everyone their free agency and will only soften someone else's heart if they are willing. For example, Moroni "prayed unto the Lord that he would give unto the Gentiles grace, that they might have charity." Then the Lord answered, "If they have not charity it mattereth not unto thee, thou has been faithful; wherefore, thy garments shall be made clean. And because thou has seen thy weakness thou shalt be made strong" (Ether 12:36–37).

We know that if we "humble ourselves and come unto him" he will make our own weaknesses become strong unto us (Ether 12:27). On the other hand, we do not know that he will make someone else's weaknesses become strong for us so that we can get along with that person better. The scriptures seem to show that sometimes he does and sometimes he doesn't—probably based on the other person's degree of willingness to respond to the Lord's spiritual promptings. The scriptural examples often show a lot of time passing and a lot of effort being made in the process of softening someone else's heart.

Nevertheless, many bear witness that heavenly help has softened the hearts of husbands and wives and helped heal relationships. Prayer helped Peggy and I turn our marriage around. One night, in response to prayer, the Lord blessed me with a greater understanding than I had ever known. I had never been a listener in our family.

It just wasn't part of my nature. My new perspective was granted in February of 1982. I was a graduate student at Brigham Young University pursuing a master's degree in counseling. My wife and I had been married for seven years, and we lived in a tiny trailer with our three children. I felt burdened by schoolwork and school loans. I also felt a rising resentment toward my lovely wife because I thought she was failing in her homemaking responsibilities. I voiced my disappointment freely, but though I didn't know it, my fault-finding was driving a big wedge between us.

At about this same time, I began my observation and counseling lab, which required me to make fourteen audio counseling tapes to submit for review. Since the first tape would be due the next week and I didn't know anyone in the program, I asked Peggy to be my counselee. I thought it would be easy to demonstrate a few listening skills on tape with someone I already knew.

We arranged a special time for me to test my listening skills on her after the kids had gone to bed. I was tense because this would be the first actual counseling tape I would submit for evaluation. Peggy had come home late that night from a church meeting and we were both tired. At first she wanted to delay the session, but the tape was due the next morning so we prayed and asked Heavenly Father to bless and inspire our efforts, then proceeded. Over the years I've come to see just how well that prayer was answered.

Peggy started hesitatingly to talk about our oldest son. She described some of the discipline problems she was having with him, and as she continued, I grew more and more frustrated. I couldn't understand why she kept talking about these problems when the whole situation seemed so simple to me. We'd gone over this same subject so many times before in arguments, and the temptation to "set her straight" was powerful. It was like a force welling up from someplace deep inside pushing me to correct or direct her. I prayed fervently for divine help to keep still, and as I persisted, I felt a quieting influence enable me to hear what she was saying and understand her feelings. I could see deeper feelings behind her words, and I was able to convey to her a sensitive understanding of those feelings. I humbly sought clarification of points that seemed unclear to me and summarized her thoughts to check my understanding. The experience was new and strange, but clearly, I was hearing her as I never had before.

There were times when she came close to tears, yet didn't cry. From time to time, her voice would break with emotion, her face would flush with feeling, her eyes would moisten with tears, and I knew she was sharing something of deep importance.

After more than forty-five minutes she seemed to be finished. I think I understood her feelings and I think she thought I understood them, so we just sat there until I said, "Let's go to bed."

I'm usually the one who prays the longest, but this time I finished my prayer before Peggy. It was a long time before she looked up, and her eyes were red and wet. We turned off the lights but just sat up a while saying nothing. Then she leaned over and said, "Steve, you've *never* listened to me like that before."

Then the Lord took that comment to my heart like an arrow, and I knew I could never be so ignorant, uncaring, and selfish again. To this day, my wife regards that event as a new beginning in our relationship, as I began to listen to her on a regular basis. I know the Lord's Spirit was with us on that night and has been with us many times since to help us through each crisis and to enrich our lives together.

Our Heavenly Father has helped parents reach rebellious children, giving them a testimony of the gospel. The prayer of faith can make a big difference in family relationships. A bishop once commented to me that things seemed to go better in his family when they were praying as a family and holding their family home evenings. Alma's example is a good example for all of us. The rebellion of his son, Alma the Younger, frustrating his father's righteous desires for him, must have caused Alma great anguish. I imagine Alma had tried everything he could think of, but it was Alma's fasting and prayers that moved the Lord to send an angel to convince his son:

> *And again, the angel said: Behold, the Lord hath heard the*
> *prayers of his people, and also the prayers of his servant, Alma,*
> *who is thy father; for he has prayed with much faith concerning*
> *thee that thou mightest be brought to the knowledge of the truth;*
> *therefore, for this purpose, have I come to convince thee of the*
> *power and authority of God, that the prayers of his servants*
> *might be answered according to their faith.* (Mosiah 27:24)

When Keith Stirling was a counselor in our stake presidency he told me this story. While he was still working at BYU and simultaneously finishing his dissertation, he was often staying up until two o'clock in the morning. During this difficult period of his life he began having special problems with his son David. He was very demanding, and their relationship was strained. Like many teenagers, he often seemed antagonistic, irresponsible, and rebellious to Brother Stirling.

David's rebellious attitude was such a trial for Brother Stirling. Once, in his frustration, he wondered about placing David in a foster home. He worried about David a lot, and in prayer he really wrestled with the Lord for guidance. Finally, in answer to his prayers, these words were put into his mind: *David has been sent here for your benefit.*

This caused Brother Stirling to question his own sour grapes attitude and to examine how much of the problem could be within himself, rather than within his son. The very thought that *he* was causing a lot of the problem wasn't easy to accept, and so he protested in his prayers, "David is the one who chose to do this and David is the one who did that, etc." He seemed able to focus only on the irresponsible or obnoxious things David was doing.

Nevertheless he couldn't shake the impression that he had been avoiding his own responsibility in this matter, so he expressed his concerns to his wife. She offered some pertinent advice, which he was open to only because of the revelation he'd received. One of her suggestions was, "Say *nothing* to David if you can't say something nice." He committed to try and was astonished at how difficult it was. He found that the first full week he could only keep his promise to his wife by not talking to David at all! Only gradually did he begin to recognize some of David's good qualities so he could mention them to his son. His wife had also suggested that David needed some affectionate physical contact, such as a touch on the arm or shoulder, hugs, etc., when talking with him. Brother Stirling was able to do this sincerely only because he had been changed himself. The Spirit had softened his heart.

David had resisted his family's desire that he serve a mission and didn't accept a mission call until a year after he was eligible. When David did decide to go on a mission, he said, "Dad, I don't know what happened, but you changed one hundred and eighty degrees. I couldn't stay mad at you because I knew that you loved me."

The prompting that David was sent to this home to bless this father was literally fulfilled. Brother Stirling said, "I learned from my experiences with David that whenever I received rebellious and angry responses from my kids, it just might mean I needed to spend more time with them or change my own attitude. I'm so grateful I learned in time. David loved his mission service so much that he served an extra two months before returning home. While there he achieved virtually every goal he set for the Lord and taught me much about faith and its processes. He has been one of the greatest blessings of my life."9

Regardless of the root cause of the problem, prayer is a powerful force we can use to help our children—and often the only source of help we can turn to. When Brother Stirling was a bishop, a mother in his ward came to him and said her fourteen-year-old daughter had run away to California and it was probably her intent to join a prostitution ring. She had been consistently rebellious—crawling out of her bedroom window late at night, shaving the sides of her head in a punk hairstyle, etc.

Bishop Stirling felt there was nothing they could do except pray. While kneeling together, he pled for this girl's well-being, asking that someone would challenge this girl and reach her in a moment of truth so that her heart would be softened.

After their prayer, the mother returned home, but called within three hours to report that her daughter had called and wanted to come home. The parents wired her the money and she returned. While this was only the first step in a difficult process, the mother felt that her daughter's change of heart was a direct answer to their prayer.[10]

Still, many faith-filled prayers of faithful parents do not result in such immediate changes. It is important to remember that the individual being prayed for maintains his free agency and makes his own choice of how to respond to increased spiritual influence brought about by prayers. But what wonderful miracles can be brought about when righteous responses are chosen to the spiritual help that we can pray into each others' lives.

Sometimes the miracle brought about by faithful prayer is not a complete change of life, but simply a reassurance that there is hope. My wife's friend had a son on drugs who ran away and had been gone for months. She feared for his life and had been praying fervently that if he were alive, he would somehow let her know. Later she also asked Peggy and some of her other friends to unite their faith and prayers that her son would call and let her know he was still alive. He called the next day.

Our Heavenly Father can change our hearts in so many ways.

Perhaps his most important change would be to fill our hearts with love. How would the pure love of Christ affect marriages? How could it affect our family relationships and our friendships? And what could it do for our relationship with God? Heavenly Father can help us resolve anger and learn to forgive. He can reveal ways to work out problems so neither partner is hurt or offended. He has great power to heal broken hearts, broken homes, and broken or endangered relationships when both parties are willing to respond to his Spirit. Jesus said that Heavenly Father had sent him to "heal the broken-hearted" (Luke 4:18). He can restore love which is vital for happy relationships.

He can change hard and unbelieving hearts.

During my five years as an active-duty Navy chaplain, our battalion's executive officer was the most intimidating Marine I ever met (and I had met many intimidating Marines). He stood over six feet tall and weighed more than 200 pounds. He shaved his head every day and wore wire rim glasses with tinted lenses. His imposing stature and his threatening stare warned everyone to obey or suffer the consequences. He was a man of commitment, and I learned to respect and like him, but when he said "No," that's exactly what he meant. Once he made up his mind, I never saw him change it.

Except once.

I had asked him to participate in presenting two worship services, just prior to our six-month deployment in the Pacific. He refused in no uncertain terms by saying, "There's no way I'm going to participate in either the prayer breakfast or the battalion Sunday service. I live an hour's drive from here, and I'd have to get up at four o'clock in the morning to make the prayer breakfast. As for Sunday's service, I spend more time here at the base now than I want to. I get precious little time with my wife, and Sunday is one of the few days I have with her. My wife has been trying to get me to go to church for years and I haven't gone yet." In curiosity, I asked him why he didn't attend, but he made a caustic remark about priests and refused to discuss it further.

I wanted to forget his refusal and choose someone else, but the Spirit pressed me to ask him again. So I knelt in prayer and told Heavenly Father, "I know the major is a tough, crusty Marine, but I really think his presentation would add to the worship services, and I *know* you can soften his heart if you want to. If it is thy will, please soften his heart so that he'll agree to give the unit history this Sunday."

Then I walked into his office and with my biggest smile said, "Sir, I didn't think up this invitation as a ruse to get you to church. I honestly think you would do the best job. I'd really like you to give a brief history of the unit this Sunday."

He didn't reply right away, but thought awhile, then leaned back in his chair and with a sheepish grin said, "Okay, I'll do it, *and* I'll be at the prayer breakfast too."

When he said that, I pressed for more, "Sir, if you're going to be there anyway, I'd like you to welcome the troops and conduct the program."

He said, "What is a welcome?"

I said, "I don't know for sure, but I copied one from another program and I think it goes something like this . . ." Then I gave him some ideas about how to do it.

He said, "Okay, I'll do it."

That night I wrote in my journal: "MIRACLE? ANSWER TO A PRAYER?" Since he had given his word, he did in fact attend both services and later commented after each one that they were the best worship services he'd ever attended. He also attended some church services on board ship while our unit was later deployed for six months.

Consider also the example of Stanislav Levchenko, a Russian

KGB spy. He was an atheist whose heart was changed when God's help was so evident that he had to recognize it. He was converted to Christianity by watching Christians pray. One of his assignments was to show visitors the cultural centers of Russia, which included churches. He would sit quietly while Russian Orthodox priests led his visitors through their churches. As people came in to pray he began to watch their faces. He said, "Sometimes their faces would be drawn and anguished, sometimes worried and scared. What always astounded me was that, once they had knelt in prayer, their faces would clear, their brows would smooth out. By the time they'd get up to leave, they looked serene, even happy. It was a phenomenon I never tired of watching." Gradually Levchenko began to see the truth, and he said, "Little by little I began to believe in the God who gave solace to people who asked for help." Levchenko's new belief and his prayers apparently led him to freedom here in America.[11]

God will help us serve him.

There is no work in which we can more confidently seek God's miraculous assistance than in his own service, the saving of souls. "Remember the worth of souls is great in the sight of God" (D&C 18:10). This work requires godlike characteristics: "And if you have not faith, hope, and charity, you can do nothing" (D&C 18:19). Only when we have the faith to bring God's Spirit into his work will he make mighty changes in people's hearts. "Verily I say unto you, he that is ordained of me and sent forth to preach the word of truth by the Comforter, in the Spirit of truth, doth he preach it by the Spirit of truth or some other way? And if it be by some other way it is not of God" (D&C 50:17–18).

When we teach by the Spirit of truth, we are doing God's work in his own way. When Herschel Pedersen was a stake missionary, he was especially interested in baptizing a certain investigator. Brother Pedersen and his companion had been giving this man the lessons and were excited because they thought the man was close to joining the Church. In his excitement Brother Pedersen fasted and prayed and spent about fifteen hours preparing a special lesson he thought would convert his investigator.

Then they went to the man's home and Brother Pedersen started giving this man his *big* lesson. Soon they could see that the *big* lesson was actually turning this man's heart away from them. Their investigator was plainly wishing they were someplace else. Brother Pedersen asked this investigator's forgiveness, candidly admitting that in assuming his big lesson was going to convert this man, he had forgotten to seek the Lord's will. Brother Pedersen asked for this man's permission to pray with him before they left. The man clearly wanted to see them go and quickly agreed in order to get them out of his home.

When they knelt in prayer, Brother Pedersen uttered just a few simple words. He asked the Lord to forgive him and his companion for being unprepared to teach what the Lord wanted taught there. Then he asked our Heavenly Father to let the Holy Ghost witness to the family that the things they had tried to teach were true. Then they left.

The next day the wife of this investigator called Brother Pedersen and said her husband wanted to be baptized. Brother Pedersen was so surprised that he asked her to reaffirm what he thought he had heard. That night, Brother Pedersen and his companion returned to this home to find out what had changed the man's mind. He said, "When you left, the Holy Ghost came, and I sat in that chair till two o'clock in the morning, and my wife and I enjoyed the presence and the comfort and the teachings of the Holy Ghost!" So Brother Pedersen and his companion had someone to baptize, but only because the Spirit intervened. He learned again that it is only the Spirit that converts.12

The scriptural record says that the people converted by Ammon and his brethren "according to the spirit of revelation and of prophecy, and the power of God working miracles in them . . . never did fall away" (Alma 23:6). When people are touched by the Lord's Spirit, they are moved in a powerful way.

Our Heavenly Father has made special promises to those who serve him. Once he said, "I will open the hearts of the people, and they will receive you. And I will establish a church by your hand" (D&C 31:7). "And again, I will visit and soften their hearts, many of them for your good, that ye may find grace in their eyes" (D&C 124:9). My parents recently returned from a mission to the Indians on a Canadian reservation. At their homecoming they told about a nonmember named Bertha who had two grandchildren. She had allowed Mom and Dad to teach her grandchildren and baptize them, but she was an angry woman who condemned and resented the smallest social infractions. Her constant anger and rejection of people made it difficult for my parents to be comfortable in her presence.

One day the children had gotten into trouble at school, and Bertha told my parents that it was because they had joined the Church. Therefore, she refused to let her grandchildren come to church or associate with the missionaries anymore. They agreed not to bother her, but the Spirit prompted them to resume their efforts, and they fasted and prayed in her behalf. That Sunday, Bertha showed up at church and brought her grandchildren with her. She had never attended church with her grandchildren previously. My parents were guided in their work with her, and she eventually overcame her anger, saying she knew she needed to learn to forgive others and drop her resentment. When my parents left, my father said she was accepting them so warmly that she almost made them feel like family members.

In addition to softening people's hearts, the Spirit can and does literally guide us step-by-step in the service of the Lord. His guidance can be remarkably precise and effective.

While Elder Glen L. Rudd presided over the old Florida

Mission, he received a letter from a young sister living in Santiago, Dominican Republic, a city with a population at that time of about 200,000 persons. This sister thought she was the only Church member in the country. She had cancer, and doctors had told her that she wouldn't live very long, so she asked if someone could come and give her a blessing.

Elder Rudd had arranged a district conference there, and so he contacted the Valentines, the one LDS family living in Santo Domingo (ninety miles south of Santiago) and asked them to take him to Santiago. Elder Rudd said he didn't realize he hadn't brought this sister's letter and didn't have her address. Elder Rudd had served as a missionary under Matthew Cowley and had learned some lessons from Elder Cowley about listening to the Spirit. He had Brother Valentine stop the car on a hill overlooking the city and listened. Then he began to give Brother Valentine directions to this sister's home as he received them from the Lord.

He directed Brother Valentine toward the congested city center and then had him turn here and there onto various roads. After some traveling in the crowded city, looking for parking, Elder Rudd told Brother Valentine that he would find a parking place at the next block if he would turn right. They found the predicted slot and slipped into it. Then Elder Rudd asked Brother Valentine to inquire about this sister. Brother Valentine went to a man leaning on a fence in front of a residence and asked him in Spanish about this sister. The surprised man said, "'Yes, she's my wife. She's just inside that door.'" Elder Rudd had directed them to a parking space in front of Sister Gomez's home in a city of 200,000 people without a map or an address—only by the power of the Spirit. They blessed her and she was healed of her cancer.[13]

The prophet Nephi said, "But behold, I say unto you that ye must pray always, and not faint; that ye must not perform any thing unto the Lord save in the first place ye shall pray unto the Father in the name of Christ, that he will consecrate thy performance unto thee, that thy performance may be for the welfare of thy soul" (2 Ne. 32:8–9). If we must not perform *any*thing unto the Lord without prayer, then how much more important is it that we do *every*thing in the Lord's service with diligent prayer and faith so that he can consecrate our performance for the welfare of our souls?

Our Heavenly Father can touch the hearts of our home teaching families, though it might take time and always depends on their free agency. He can help members of bishoprics, presidencies, and teachers. He can soften the hearts of the people we are trying to teach and influence. He can fill us with a love for all of our brothers and sisters, both in and out of the Church. He can soften their hearts toward our message. He can fill us with insight about their most pressing needs, and he will fill our most pressing needs if we *listen humbly* for his guidance and direction.

Notes

1. Spencer W. Kimball, "The False Gods We Worship," *Ensign,* June 1976, 5.
2. Norman Vincent Peale, *Positive Imaging: The Powerful Way to Change Your Life* (New York: Fawcett Crest, 1982), 51–52.
3. Orson F. Whitney, *Life of Heber C. Kimball* (Salt Lake City: Bookcraft, 1974), 272.
4. Marjorie A. McCormick, "One Shovelful of Coal," *Ensign,* October 1979, 49.
5. B. Lloyd Poelman, "Strike the Steel," *New Era,* October 1975, 26–28.
6. As told to me personally.
7. William G. Hartley, "Personal and Family Preparedness: Lessons from Church History," *Principles of the Gospel in Practice: Sperry Symposium 1985* (Salt Lake City: Randall Book, 1985), 227–29.
8. Fenton L. Williams, "Who Helped My Horse?" "Mormon Journal," *Ensign,* July 1978, 66–68.
9. Keith Stirling, as he told this story to me.
10. Ibid.
11. Stanislav Levchenko, *On the Wrong Side: My Life in the KGB* (New York: Dell Publishing, 1988), 62.
12. Herschel Pedersen, transcript of a talk.
13. Glen L. Rudd, "Keeping the Gospel Simple," BYU Devotional Talk, 16 Feb., 1988.

9

The Importance of Faith in God's Will

For my thoughts are not your thoughts, neither are your ways my ways, saith the LORD.

For as the heavens are higher than the earth, so are my ways higher than your ways, and my thoughts than your thoughts. (Isa. 55:8)

It is inevitable that our desires will sometimes collide with God's desires because his thoughts, feelings, and intentions are infinitely higher than our own.

If we think about it, it becomes apparent that Heavenly Father would want to implant his higher spiritual hopes and desires in us because he wants us to become like him and like his Son. Jesus said, "What manner of men ought ye to be? Verily I say unto you, even as I am" (3 Ne. 27:27). The only way we can become more like our Father and his Son is through soul growth. So is it any wonder the Lord's first commitment is to our spiritual growth?

M. Scott Peck, a psychiatrist speaking about the process of psychotherapy, said that "our human spiritual growth is of the utmost importance to something greater than ourselves. This something we call God."[1] He says he has observed God's grace at work in his clients, nurturing their spiritual growth. Throughout his book, Dr. Peck stresses again and again that God's first commitment is to our spiritual growth. The Lord Jesus Christ asked, "For what shall it profit a man, if he shall gain the whole world, and lose his own soul?" (Mark 8:36). With God, our soul comes first. There are no exceptions. The apostle Paul said that we can have the gift of prophecy and all faith to move mountains, but if we don't have charity we are nothing (1 Cor. 13:2). Even spiritual gifts are ranked by their contribution to our salvation.

On one occasion, our Father spoke bluntly to the Prophet Joseph Smith in chastisement for acceding to Martin Harris's pleadings to borrow the 116 Book of Mormon manuscript pages even after the Lord had rebuffed the request.

> *For although a man may have many revelations, and have power to do many mighty works, yet if he boasts in his own strength, and sets at naught the counsels of God, and follows after the dictates of his own will and carnal desires, he must fall and incur the vengeance of a just God upon him. (D&C 3:4)*

When it comes to our spiritual growth and salvation, some things will matter to the Lord and other things will not. In response to five different inquiries of men recorded in the Doctrine & Covenants, the Lord answered: "It mattereth not to me."[2] On one of these occasions he told them to use their own judgment, and on the fifth occasion he said simply, "For ye cannot go amiss" (D&C 80:3). To other inquiries, he gave specific instructions or counsel. Once he emphasized the importance of a thing by saying, "take heed that ye see to this matter" (D&C 96:1–4). On other occasions recorded in the Doctrine and Covenants he said, basically, "Don't trouble me with this anymore."[3]

To earnestly attempt to understand and be in harmony with the Lord is a marvelous spiritual attribute worthy of the highest degree of cultivation. Such efforts bring us close to him so that little by little we begin to "know" him. Jesus said, "And this is life eternal, that they might know thee the only true God, and Jesus Christ, whom thou hast sent" (John 17:3). The Book of Mormon tells of the prophet Nephi, who lived at the time Christ visited America and sought to do the Lord's will continually, even through some especially difficult circumstances. Eventually, the Lord told him:

> *Blessed art thou, Nephi, for those things which thou hast done; for I have beheld how thou hast with unwearyingness declared the word, which I have given unto thee, unto this people. And thou hast not feared them, and hast not sought thine own life, but hast sought my will, and to keep my commandments.*
>
> *And now, because thou hast done this with such unwearyingness, behold, I will bless thee forever; and I will make thee mighty in word and in deed, in faith and in works; yea, even that all things shall be done unto thee according to thy word, for thou shalt not ask that which is contrary to my will.* (Hel. 10:4–5)

In the presence of angels, our Heavenly Father gave Nephi power to move mountains because he knew Nephi would ask nothing contrary to his will (Hel. 10:6–10). Our Heavenly Father loves those who trust in his *will* as much as they trust in his power. Our Savior Jesus Christ is a perfect example. He said: "I can of mine own self do nothing: as I hear, I judge: and my judgment is just; because I seek not mine own will, but the will of the Father which hath sent me" (John 5:30). Even Heavenly Father's infinite love for Jesus, his Only Begotten Son, did not change his will. He still refused the Savior's request to let the cup pass from him in the Garden of Gethsemane (Luke 22:42) because of his love for all of us. From this divine example, it must be clear that Heavenly Father is going to see matters from a higher plane, and thus his feelings will often be different than our own feelings.

Even though Heavenly Father can answer our prayers immediately and often does, his answer may be "No" or "Not now." When I was a missionary, a sister in a ward in which I was serving told us that her husband had been beaten and robbed by three men on Hollywood Boulevard, leaving him dependent on her for care. Sometimes he was able to walk with a cane, but at other times he suffered headaches and convulsions and could not walk at all. This couple had been converted to the Church many years earlier and had a very strong faith. Many times they had experienced miraculous healings through priesthood blessings. Consequently, when her husband's injuries from the beating were life-threatening, they felt certain the Lord would heal him. His life was saved by a blessing, but they sought another from their bishop for a complete recovery. Their bishop laid his hands on this brother's head and blessed him with strength to bear his infirmity, but he gave no blessing for complete recovery.

They asked why, and the bishop responded, "I felt impressed that it was not the Lord's will that this affliction be lifted from him." That answer disappointed them, and a few months later they sought a blessing for complete recovery from their stake president. The stake president and his counselors fasted and prayed with them before the blessing. Nevertheless, his blessing was in substance identical to the bishop's blessing.

Still, this good sister and her husband hoped for a complete recovery. When a General Authority whom they both knew visited the area for a stake conference, they contacted him and requested a blessing, not mentioning the previous blessings. He, too, laid his hands upon this good brother's head and gave essentially the same blessing the bishop and stake president had given. After the blessing, he said, "The Lord isn't going to grant a complete recovery, and I know he has told you this in previous blessings. You shouldn't trifle with his answer, even if you don't understand it. He loves you and will provide strength and comfort sufficient for your needs." This sister confirmed that the Lord had strengthened them greatly and that although there had been hard times, there had been more good times.

The apostle Paul said the Lord gave him a thorn in the flesh and that he besought the Lord for healing three times. He said he stopped asking because the Lord told him, "My grace is sufficient for thee: for my strength is made perfect in weakness." So he shifted his attitude to gratitude so "that the power of Christ" could rest more fully upon him (2 Cor. 12:7–9). Paul knew our Father loved him, and we can have that same strength. Knowing that God will help us through sore trials should blast away the notion that we are meaningless or insignificant to him. Recognizing his help should help us see that we live under the caring, watchful eyes of God, "not at the periphery but at the center of His vision, His concern."4

One of my favorite country songs is "Unanswered Prayers." Garth Brooks sings the story of how a married couple run into the husband's old high school sweetheart. Their meeting reminds the husband of how he had once prayed daily for that earlier love to last forever and told God he'd never ask for anything else. But meeting his old flame now, years later, he knows that God knew what he was doing all along. As she walks away, he looks at his wife and thanks God for her and "unanswered prayers."5

At other times we may think Heavenly Father has not answered or has said no, but he is simply answering according to his own timing. Even though such answers may come slowly we can be certain God always answers with compassion. The Lord once gave the brother of Jared a special blessing and said, "And thus will I do unto thee because this long time ye have cried unto me" (Ether 1:43). How long do we need to continue our faith if we know our request is worthy and does not run counter to God's will? That's a judgment call requiring spiritual discernment.

Abraham and his wife Sarah asked the Lord for children for many years, yet Sarah did not conceive and have a child until her time for child-bearing was well past. She was in her nineties when she bore their only child, Isaac. Abraham and Sarah received their blessings because they kept their faith throughout trials which lasted for a very long time.

It may take a lot of time before we find out why God has answered us in certain ways. We may never understand God's reasons while in mortality, but we can still press on, knowing his love is real, that he always watches over us and cares for us, and whatever he does is for our best good.

Art Berg's marvelous book *Some Miracles Take Time* helped me understand more clearly than any other book I have ever read why God allows us to suffer. In this book he shares his own exquisite trials. When he was twenty-one years old, he was sleeping en route from California to Utah where he was to complete preparations for his marriage. The driver fell asleep at the wheel and the car rolled. The accident broke Art's neck, left him a quadriplegic, and cut short his dreams. He suffered enormously during his stay in the hospital, especially when his doctor clamped the halo brace on his head and screwed the bolts into his skull, but the Lord sustained him and became much more real to him.

After his marriage, his paralysis contributed to heavy burdens and trials for his wife, Dallas, and one night Dallas felt particularly discouraged. As she finished placing the dishes in the cupboard, the top shelf collapsed on the shelves below, leaving her standing tearfully in a mess of broken dishes. She cried for a full thirty minutes and tried to call her mom, then her sister, and then her best friend, hoping for sympathy. Since they weren't home, she prayed instead. Through prayer and patience, she experienced gradually increasing levels of strength and tolerance and said, "Looking back, my former concerns seem trivial to me. I have come so far and things that were hard for me then are easy for me now."[6] Isn't this one way our Father can make weak things become strong unto us? The Lord did not relieve their burdens, but replaced weakness with strength.

Art and Dallas testify that God created miracle after miracle in their lives. Some years later, Art is still not walking, though that was promised to him in a priesthood blessing. Even so, he continues to exercise his faith and prayers and limbs, knowing that God has already created countless other miracles for him. I heard him speak at a stake fireside, and it was a marvelous experience to be there. At that time he seemed to have acquired an amazing control of his upper body, and I could not tell that he was quadriplegic. He was still in a wheelchair, but he was using his arms with strength and grace. Elder Boyd K. Packer has said, "Some people think a miracle is only a miracle if it happens instantaneously, but miracles can grow slowly and patience and faith can compel things to happen that otherwise never would have come to pass."[7] Art believes the miracle he was promised of the use of his legs is taking time but is proceeding according to the Lord's timetable and will eventually come.

Even though our Heavenly Father may not answer our righteous prayers immediately, it is important to remember that the Lord can help us in many different ways. Our Heavenly Father can give us marvelous strength to endure. He can lighten our burdens so that we cannot feel them. He once told his followers who were slaves to the Lamanites: "I will also ease the burdens which are put upon your shoulders, even that you cannot feel them upon your backs" (Mosiah 24:14). The scriptures record that he kept his promise and then later set them free in his own time and in his own way.

The apostle Paul itemized some of the sufferings experienced by the early Saints and said that the Lord had provided some better things for them through their sufferings, for without sufferings they could not be made perfect (See JST Heb. 11:40). He also said that even though Christ was God's Son, yet he learned "obedience by the things which he suffered" (Heb. 5:8). Hosea said of Israel that "in their affliction they will seek me early" (Hosea 5:15). Paul said "that we must through much tribulation enter into the kingdom of God" (Acts 14:22).

The most difficult of trials have the potential of producing deeply ingrained faith. The poignant testimony of a handcart pioneer illustrates this principle beautifully. An elderly gentleman sat in a Sunday School class listening to the teacher criticize Church leaders for letting the Martin Handcart Company begin its journey so late in the year. Finally the elderly man arose and said in great sincerity:

> I ask you to stop this criticism. You are discussing a matter you know nothing about. Cold historic facts mean nothing here, for they give no proper interpretation of the questions involved. Mistake to send the Handcart Company out so late in the season? Yes. But I was in that company and my wife was in it and Sister Nellie Unthank, whom you have cited, was there, too. We suffered beyond anything you can imagine and many died of exposure and starvation, but did you ever hear a survivor of that company utter a word of criticism? No one of that company ever apostatized [sic] or left the Church, because everyone of us came through with the absolute knowledge that God lives for we became acquainted with him in our extremities.
>
> I have pulled my handcart when I was so weak and weary from illness and lack of food that I could hardly put one foot ahead of the other. I have looked ahead and seen a patch of sand or a hill slope and I have said, I can go only that far and there I must give up, for I cannot pull the load through it. . . . I have gone on to that sand and when I reached it, the cart

began pushing me. I have looked back many times to see who was pushing my cart, but my eyes saw no one. I knew then that the angels of God were there.

Was I sorry that I chose to come by handcart? No. Neither then nor any minute of my life since. The price we paid to become acquainted with God was a privilege to pay, and I am thankful that I was privileged to come in the Martin Handcart Company.[8]

This gallant brother asks us to refrain from judging the Lord and to consider instead how our Father built his faith, steadfastness, and charity. He mentioned looking back many times to see who was pushing the cart. That may seem unreal, yet Dallas Berg testified herself of receiving such divine physical assistance not long ago.

She described a time when her arm was nearly useless from an injury, and she stood at the rear of her hatchback in a white dress, in the rain. Her frustration mounted as she wondered how she could possibly lift Art's heavy wheelchair into the car trunk while holding up the hatchback lid and an umbrella *when she had only one good arm.* She put the umbrella down, and with her good arm she opened the hatchback and held it up. Then she extended her injured arm to try to lift the wheelchair. She said, "Suddenly, I felt invisible hands lifting also. The chair felt light as a feather—as did my burden. The chair slid into the trunk with no effort at all. Now my tears were of gratitude."[9]

Affliction can teach us compassion for others. William Hurt starred in a movie called *The Doctor,* in which he played a proud and insensitive surgeon who developed a cancer in his throat. As he suffered from both his cancer and his own doctor's insensitive treatment, he began to see the pain of his own patients, and he developed deep compassion for them as they suffered. His own suffering made him a much better doctor. The story was based on the true experience of Ed Rosenbaum, M.D., who wrote of it in his book, *A Taste of My Own Medicine.* If you see the movie, you can't fail to see the principle.

The scriptures seem to indicate that suffering and adversity, if we endure them well, can build great strength, compassion, and faith into the core of our souls. One family I know is full of faith, and when their daughter contracted scoliosis, which curves the spine laterally and is potentially crippling, they prayed fervently with great faith that she would be healed, but she wasn't. That surprised them because they had experienced many previous healings in the family, some of them marvelous and instantaneous. They prayed that an operation would not be necessary and first tried having her wear a mechanical brace which was molded from her hips to her head and lengthened weekly to stretch her spine. She wore it twenty-three hours a day for a full year. In spite of this, an operation *became* necessary. So they prayed that the surgeon's hands would be guided and assisted by the Lord while he operated on their daughter.

After the operation the doctor said, "I do an average of six of these operations each week in Utah and California and she has responded better than any patient I have ever had. She is my number one patient."

In time their daughter was made completely well. They said they wondered why God had chosen such a painful way to heal their daughter until they saw her "develop a great empathy for others in pain, and become the most compassionate person you can imagine."[10] This was better than a simple healing because God cannot give a greater gift to us than compassion for others.

The prophet Moroni said that charity "is the pure love of Christ, and it endureth forever; and whoso is found possessed of it at the last day, it shall be well with him" (Moro. 7:47). I know of no other gift which will have more value when we stand at the judgment bar of God. Remember, the apostle Paul said that without it, we are nothing. Alma said that "if ye do not remember to be charitable, ye are as dross, which the refiners do cast out, (it being of no worth) and is trodden under foot of men" (Alma 34:28–29).

Sometimes it can appear as though God has not granted our desire, when in fact he is planning to respond with a better answer. A teenager wrote that she had been traumatized socially in the fifth grade when her only two friends suddenly became her enemies. They harassed her with prank phone calls and succeeded in getting others to mock her. They even passed around a notebook exclusively for others to write put-downs against her. All through junior high school she endured a haunting loneliness. The result was that she didn't expect any new friendship to endure.

Then in high school a new student was assigned to the locker next to hers and they became best friends. Everything was going well, until one day, her friend showed up with a girl who had just moved in. She instantly feared she would lose her friend to this new girl. In her prayers, she vented her anger on the Lord, accusing him of letting her down. She pleaded with the Lord to do something—such as turn her friend and the newcomer against each other—so she would retain her friend.

Much to her surprise, the new girl became her friend too—as though they had been friends all their lives. She said, "When you pray for something, God sometimes gives you *more* than you ask for."[11]

Sometimes, when we make a prayer request, our Heavenly Father will assign us special homework or require something of us before he acts. Elder Gene R. Cook had received a very special set of scriptures from his parents when he was a young man. His parents had placed sacred inscriptions in them, and he had invested countless hours indexing and marking important verses in them. These scriptures were the only earthly possessions he valued significantly. Many times he had told his wife that in the event of a fire, besides his family those scriptures were all he cared about saving.

When they were stolen from a locked van at an airport in Bolivia, Elder Cook initiated herculean search efforts. The mission did everything in their power to find the scriptures—even offering a reward in the newspaper. Everyone present in the mission home knelt daily and pled for their return in a way which would bring someone into the Church.

During this time Elder Cook felt disheartened and lost his desire to study the Lord's word. Three weeks passed without his receiving any news of his scriptures. Then came a burning spiritual impression. He was asked how long he was going to neglect searching the scriptures.

Admittedly this prompting gave no direct guidance to his scriptures, but it turned out to be like Elisha's direction to the Syrian general, Naaman. Elder Cook began reading and cross-referencing another set of scriptures—thus he did God's homework assignment. Within a few days, a friend brought in his scriptures with some other valuable mission papers. God had miraculously lifted them from thieves in La Paz and returned them intact. Both the woman who returned them and her son were baptized.[12]

In this book, I have pointed out that we might lack sufficient humility, gratitude, or faith to receive a miracle. Lacking something in these qualities is probably our most common failing. It's also true that our desire or request can simply be unworthy. Ammon represented the Lord well when he said to King Lamoni, "Whatsoever thou desirest *which is right,* that will I do" (Alma 18:17; emphasis mine). God knows us and our real needs and always looks out for our long-term welfare, ranking our spiritual growth ahead of our physical welfare. That's why he'll bring about a famine to humble us, if necessary (see Hel. 11).

Often our Heavenly Father can nurture our growth better by letting us work through our difficulties. Our Heavenly Father often chooses to intervene in subtle, rather than obvious, ways. He often does the smallest thing possible to produce the greatest righteous effect. We need to start looking for his grace in the small but sublime events that occur in our lives every day. In referring to the miracle of the Liahona, different prophets said:

> *And thus we see that by small means the Lord can bring about great things. (1 Ne. 16:29; see also verses 10, 23–31)*
>
> *Now ye may suppose that this is foolishness in me; but behold I say unto you, that by small and simple things are great things brought to pass; and small means in many instances doth confound the wise.*
>
> *And the Lord God doth work by small means to bring about his great and eternal purposes; and by very small means the Lord doth confound the wise and bringeth about the salvation of many souls. (Alma 37:6–7; see also verses 41, 38–45)*

In summary, we might call this step developing faith in the Lord's *will*. We are trusting that he knows what is best for us and what will best develop our personal growth, power, and strength. It requires wisdom just to desire this kind of faith. However, I know of at least one great leader in the world who testifies of its value. John Templeton borrowed $10,000 to start a mutual fund which has now grown into a group which, in 1987, was managing at least six billion dollars for more than a half-million investors. He is considered a great leader in the investment field. During the middle of his life, his faith in God was rejuvenated and he began the practice of prayer in all his affairs. But he doesn't pray for success or wealth. He prays instead that God will use him to bless others. He does not believe prayer was meant for selfish goals, and he often simply asks that our Father's will be done.[13]

In a way his prayer is similar to Solomon's. The Lord promised Solomon his heart's desire, and Solomon asked simply for God's wisdom in his responsibilities. This so pleased the Lord that he also gave Solomon immeasurable riches and glory (see 1 Kgs. 3:7–14). It isn't likely that Heavenly Father is going to make us rich because we pray for his will to be done, but that's not the point. Think about your own children. Suppose one of them approached you with a request but then added with total sincerity, "Dad, please do what you think is best. I trust your judgment." That would be marvelous faith to see in a child and very heart-warming. Could you withhold yourself from such a son or daughter without a very good reason?

When I think of the Savior healing the sick and afflicted wherever he found sufficient faith, I get the distinct impression that our Heavenly Father wants to heal and bless his children. Elder F. Enzio Busche contracted an incurable liver disease as a young man. He reached a point when he thought his life would end in a few days and yet unanswered questions about life raged in his soul. He saw no way out of his despair when there came a clear spiritual impression: "If you pray now, you will regain your health."[14]

There were many things he could have said. He could have asked for his life, but instead, he simply acceded to the Lord's will. In the instant he spoke, a strength entered his soul and filled him with a certainty of his recovery and an unspeakable joy. He committed himself to keep the memory of his divine experience forever, and he also committed himself to consciously strive to understand and serve God, who had healed him.

His condition improved so dramatically that his doctors considered it a miracle. Even so, his father pressed them to perform an exploratory surgery. To everyone's surprise, the surgery revealed that Elder Busche had developed a healthy new liver, just like an infant's, with no scarring from his sickness.

Most of the time, I think Heavenly Father wants to heal us and simply waits for our faith. Mormon encouraged us: "Be wise . . . ask not, that ye may consume it upon your lusts, but ask with a firmness unshaken, that ye will yield to no temptation, but that ye will serve the true and living God" (Morm. 9:28). We need to learn that becoming like our Father in Heaven is the best miracle we can seek.

It is possible, even likely, to make the crucial error of assuming that everything that happens is God's will, so there is nothing to pray about. This mistaken form of thinking assumes that because God allows a circumstance, he created it or wants it and will refuse to change it. That assumption is a crucial error because it keeps us from exercising our faith to receive his miracles. It causes us to assume that he won't act in our behalf.

It may be true on some occasions that it is God's will to allow a trial or infirmity to remain with us—such as in the case of the beaten brother who was not totally healed—but surely it is not true on every occasion, and we can generally learn God's will only through heartfelt prayer. As God's children, we seek his will so seldom that our laziness has been observed even in psychotherapy by psychiatrist M. Scott Peck, who said that "human beings routinely fail to obtain God's side of the issue . . . because we are lazy."[15]

When Lehi shared his dream of the tree of life, Nephi sought and received an interpretation from the Lord, who sent an angel to explain it. Later he found his brothers Laman and Lemuel grumbling and wondering about the dream. When he asked them, "Have ye inquired of the Lord?" they said, "We have not; for the Lord maketh no such thing known unto us." To this response, Nephi replied:

> *How is it that ye do not keep the commandments of the Lord?*
>
> *Do ye not remember the things which the Lord hath said?—If ye will not harden your hearts, and ask me in faith, believing that ye shall receive, with diligence in keeping my commandments, surely these things shall be made known unto you. (1 Ne. 15:8–11)*

If our request is based on good intentions, it really doesn't hurt to ask. It is a fair assumption that requesting something good will not collide with Heavenly Father's will. We just need to stop our request if Heavenly Father so directs us. President Romney said he and his wife prayed about a thing for years, but stopped asking when they learned it was not our Father's will. Even our Savior asked in the Garden of Gethsemane for his suffering to be lifted, but he said and meant, "Nevertheless not my will, but thine be done" (Luke 22:42).

Sometimes we simply lose our desire for the thing we have been requesting. For more than a year, I asked my family to pray that I would be transferred into the data processing section of the National Guard in Draper. I thought my reasons were pretty good because the unit did not leave the area for its summer training but worked right there at the headquarters building in Draper. Such an assignment would allow me to remain home with my family during the summer. Even so, I made sure the Lord understood that I wanted his will to be done and not mine. I never did get the transfer, but instead, I lost my desire for the move as I grew to enjoy the soldiers in my unit more and more.

As we pursue our Father's will, we should expect *more* miracles, not fewer. Although the Lord did not grant my transfer, he helped me retire two years earlier than I had thought possible. This enabled me to stay home at a crucial time, a miracle I had not thought to ask for.

No one ever pursued his Father's will with more dedication than our Lord, Jesus Christ, and think of the innumerable miracles done through him. John the Beloved said there were so "many other things which Jesus did, the which, if they should be written every one, I suppose that even the world itself could not contain the books that should be written" (John 21:25).

Even though God may not grant the specific miracle we desire, he may grant another, even many others. So look for a lot of miracles and learn to recognize them when they come, for as President Kimball himself said, there are "infinitely more miracles today than in any age past and just as wondrous."[16]

❦

A Personal Note

As a conclusion, I feel impressed to note that the very work of writing this book has changed my prayers, my attitude about miracles, and the way I think about Heavenly Father.

I find myself listening more and seeking his will. I find myself wanting more and more to know what he thinks and how he feels. Though I still make specific requests and still find them answered, I find myself less concerned when the answer is either delayed or is a clear refusal.

Perhaps that is why I re-emphasized this last chapter. Is it possible that the most important results of prayer are those sublime changes which it produces within our very own souls? How do these intimate conversations change us? I know that the time I have spent in conversation with my wife and family has changed me greatly. That being so, what are the effects of intimate conversations with God which continue over long periods of time?

If you knew me before I thought prayer had any real value, when I prayed only because I was commanded, then you might think the effects have been remarkable. Please don't misunderstand me. I am not perfect and I have never intended this book to be the last word on prayer. But I know that this miraculous gift of conversing with our deeply loving Father is one of my most precious experiences, for it is in prayer that I most often find myself thinking, "my cup runneth over."

I challenge you to seek out and discover prayer's treasured blessings.

In the movie *Shadowlands,* C.S. Lewis's wife is dying of cancer and he prays fervently to God. She receives a remission from her cancer, and the Oxford chaplain is ecstatic, thinking Lewis has received the miracle he must have sought. But Lewis chides him, saying, "That's not why I pray, Harry. I pray because I can't help myself. I pray because I'm helpless. I pray because the need flows out of me all the time, waking and sleeping. It [prayer] doesn't change God. It changes me."[17]

And surely that inner change of heart must be the most important miracle of all.

Notes

1. M. Scott Peck, *The Road Less Travelled: A New Psychology of Love, Traditional Values and Spiritual Growth* (New York: Touchstone, 1978), 312.
2. Doctrine & Covenants 60:5; 61:22; 62:5; 63:40; & 80:3.
3. Doctrine & Covenants 5:29; 59:22; 90:33; & 130:15.
4. Peck, 312.
5. Pat Alger, Larry B. Bastain, & Garth Brooks, "Unanswered Prayers," *No Fences.* Compact Disc.
6. Art E. Berg, *Some Miracles Take Time* (American Fork, UT: Covenant Communications, 1990), 118.
7. In Berg, 1.
8. Ibid., 174–75.
9. Ibid., 91.
10. As told to me by Eldon & Colleen Davis.
11. Linda Neukrug, "The Triangle," *Guideposts,* March 1992, 37.
12. Gene R. Cook, *Living by the Power of Faith* (Salt Lake City: Deseret Book, 1985), 2–5.
13. In James Ellison, *The Templeton Plan: 21 Steps to Personal Success and Real Happiness* (San Francisco: A Giniger Book, 1987), vii, 131.
14. Hartman and Connie Rector, "Life's Questions Answered," *No More Strangers* (Salt Lake City: Bookcraft, 1971), 101.
15. Peck, 273. For a greater appreciation of Dr. Peck's deep psychological insight into spiritual growth, see chapter eight in this volume.
16. In Berg, 1.
17. Leonore Fleischer, *Shadowlands* (New York: A SIGNET BOOK, 1993), 198.

About the Author

Stephen M. Bird was raised in Ogden, Utah. He graduated from Brigham Young University with a master's degree in counseling and guidance. He served a mission to California in 1968-1970 and was an LDS chaplain in the Navy from 1983 to 1988.

Stephen Bird has taught a course entitled "Religion and Education" at the BYU Salt Lake Center and is a counselor at Mountain Ridge Junior High School in Highland, Utah.

His main interests are his family, the gospel, and writing. He has served in many leadership capacities in the Church, including bishop and stake high councilor, and is currently the Gospel Doctrine instructor in his ward. He and his wife, Peggy, are the parents of four children Alan, Keralyn, Justin, and Jarren. They reside in Pleasant Grove, Utah.